Onshape Tutorials

Tutorial Books

D1698831

For resource files contact us at
Online.books999@gmail.com

Table of Contents

Introduction

Welcome to *Onshape Tutorials* book. This book is written to assist students, designers, and engineering professionals in designing 3D models. It covers the essential features and functionalities of Onshape using relevant tutorials and exercises.

Topics covered in this Book

- Chapter 1, "Getting Started with Onshape," gives an introduction to Onshape. The user interface and terminology are discussed in this chapter.

- Chapter 2, "Sketch Techniques," explores the sketching commands in Onshape. You will learn to create parametric sketches.

- Chapter 3, "Extrude and Revolve features," teaches you to create basic 3D geometry using the Extrude and Revolve commands.

- Chapter 4, "Placed Features," covers the features which can be created without using sketches.

- Chapter 5, "Patterned Geometry," explores the commands to create patterned and mirrored geometry.

- Chapter 6, "Sweep Features," covers the commands to create swept and helical features.

- Chapter 7, "Loft Features," covers the Loft command and its core features.

- Chapter 8, "Additional Features," covers additional commands to create complex geometry.

- Chapter 9, "Modifying Parts," explores the commands and techniques to modify the part geometry.

- Chapter 10, "Assemblies," helps you to create assemblies using the bottom-up and top-down design approaches.

- Chapter 11, "Drawings," covers how to create 2D drawings from 3D parts and assemblies.

Chapter 1: Getting Started with Onshape

Introduction to Onshape

Onshape is a cloud-based CAD application. It is a parametric and feature-based system that allows you to create 3D parts, assemblies, and 2D drawings. The design process in Onshape is shown below.

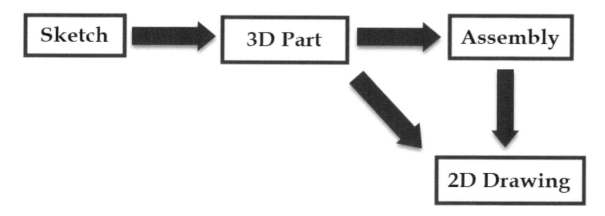

In Onshape, everything is controlled by parameters, dimensions, or constraints. For example, if you want to change the position of the hole shown in the figure, you need to change the dimension or relation that controls its position.

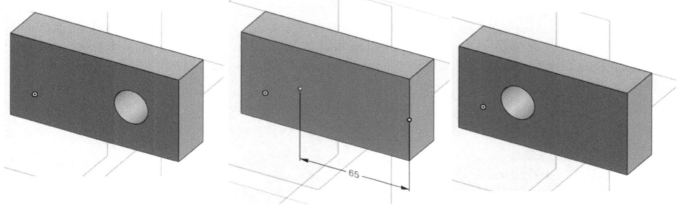

The parameters and constraints that you set up allow you to have control over the design intent. The design intent describes the way your 3D model will behave when you apply dimensions and constraints to it. For example, if you want to position the hole at the center of the block, one way is to add dimensions between the hole and the adjacent edges. However, when you change the size of the block, the hole will not be at the center.

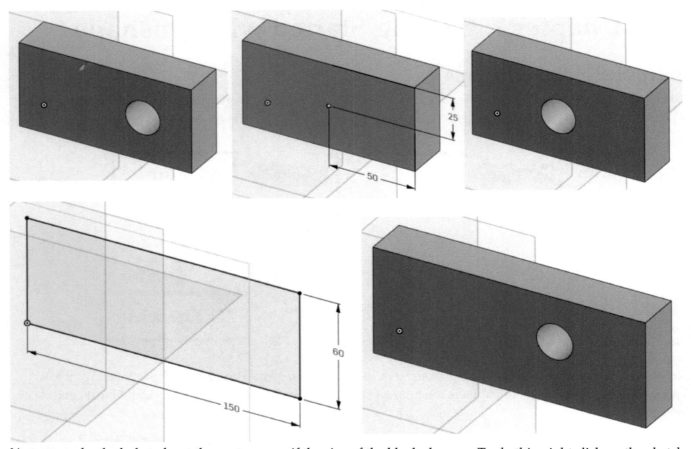

You can make the hole to be at the center, even if the size of the block changes. To do this, right click on the sketch used to create the hole and select **Edit**. Next, delete the dimensions and create a diagonal construction line. Apply the Midpoint constraint between the hole point and the diagonal construction line. Next, click the green check on the Sketch dialog.

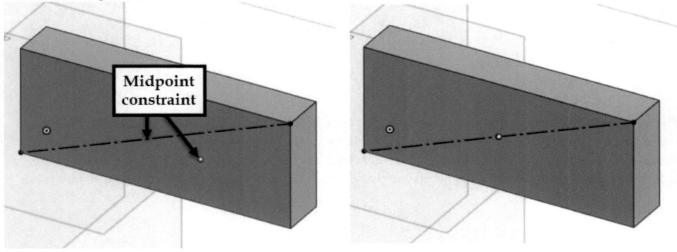

Now, even if you change the size of the block, the hole will always remain at the center.

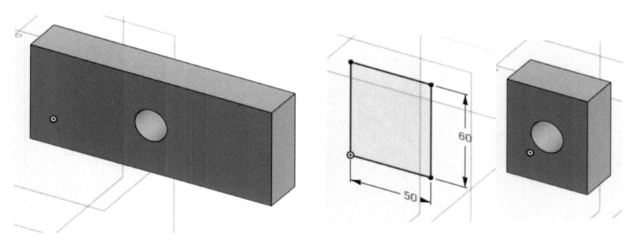

Starting Onshape

To start **Onshape**, open your internet browser and type www.onshape.com in the address bar. Next, click the **SIGN IN** button located at the top right corner. Next, enter your registered email ID and password, and then click the **Sign in** button. On the Documents page, click the **Create** button located at the top left corner, and then select **Document**. Next, enter the name of the document in the **Document name** box and click **OK**; a new design file will appear on the screen. You can change the working units of the file. To do this, click the **Document menu** located at the top left corner. Next, click the **Workspace units** option and set the **Default unit type** and click the green check.

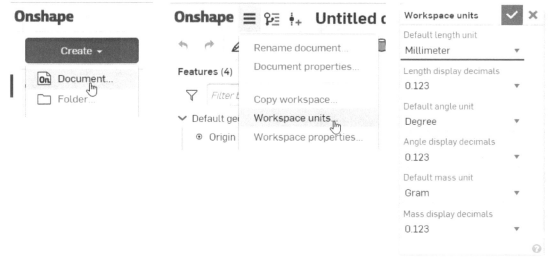

User Interface

The following image shows the **Onshape** application window.

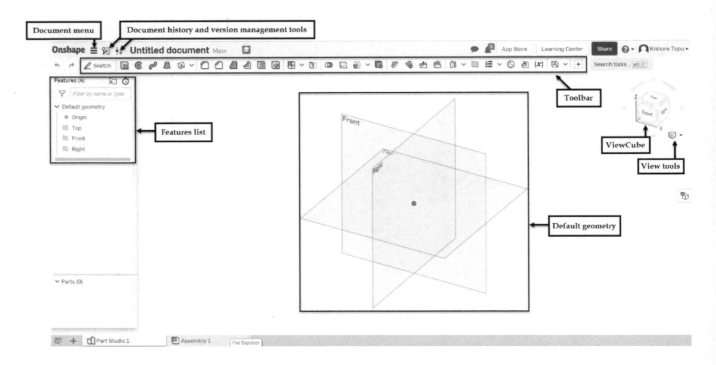

Toolbars in Onshape

There are five toolbars available in Onshape: **Document**, **Feature**, **Assembly**, **Sketch**, and **Drawing**.

The **Document** toolbar has commands to create documents, document versions, add comments, share documents, and so on.

The **Feature** toolbar has all the commands to create solid models.

This **Sketch** toolbar has commands to create sketches.

The **Assembly** toolbar has commands to assemble the parts.

The **Drawing** toolbar has all the commands to generate 2D drawings of parts and assemblies.

The other components of the user interface are discussed next.

Document menu

This is located at the top left corner of the window. It consists of commonly used commands such as **Rename document**, **Document properties**, **Copy workspace**, **Workspace units**, **Print**, and **Close document**.

Graphics area

Graphics area is the blank space located below the toolbar. You can draw sketches and create 3D geometry in the Graphics area. The left corner of the graphics area has a **Features** list. It captures the design history of the model. You can edit the sketches and features of the model using the **Features** list. In addition to that, you can Hide/Show the planes, and sketches of the 3D model.

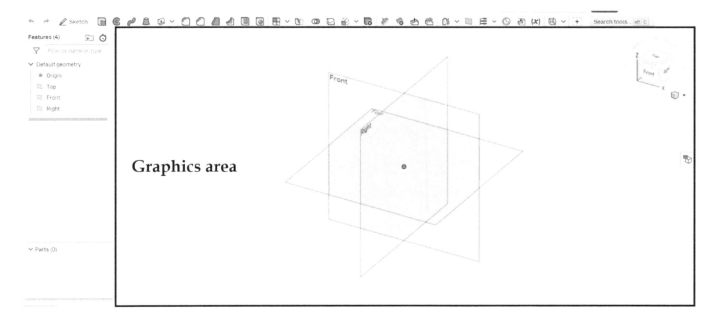

Comments dialog

The **Comments** dialog appears when you click the **Comments** icon located at the top right corner of the window.

You can add comments to the model by clicking the **Tag entity**  icon on the **Comments** dialog and selecting an entity from the graphics window. Next, enter the comments in the **Add comment** box and click the **Add** button.

You can also attach an image to the comment. To do this, click the **Browse for attachment** icon and select an image.

View Tools

The **View tools** drop-down is located below the ViewCube. It contains the tools to change the model orientation, zoom, change the visual style of the model. It also has settings to highlight the boundary edges and turn ON/OFF the section view.

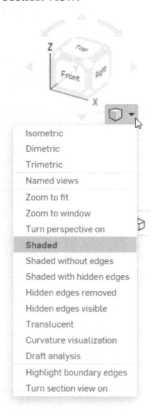

View Cube

It is located at the top right corner of the graphics area and is used to set the view orientation of the model.

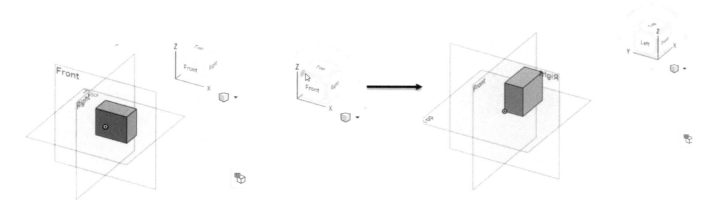

Dialogs

Dialogs are part of Onshape user interface. Using a dialog, you can easily specify many settings and options. Various components of a dialog are shown below.

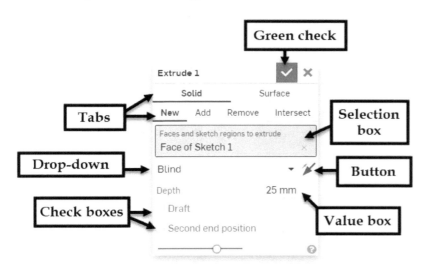

Shortcut menus

Shortcut Menus are displayed when you right-click on the graphics area. Onshape provides various shortcut menus in order to help you access some options very easily and quickly. The options in shortcut menus vary based on the workspace. In addition to that, the options in the shortcut menu depending on the selection.

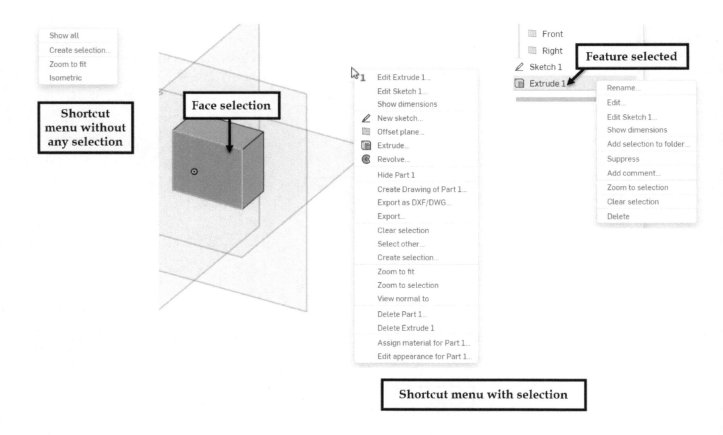

Onshape Help

Onshape offers you with the help system that goes beyond basic command definition. You can access Onshape help by clicking on the **Help menu** icon on the right side of the window.

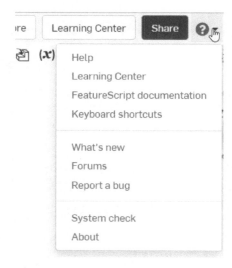

Documents page

The **Documents** page is an essential feature of Onshape. It is used to store, organize, and share the documents. You can display Documents page by clicking the **Onshape** icon located at the top left corner of the window. It displays a list of folders and documents created by you. You can create a new folder by clicking the **Create** button and select the **Folder** option. Next, enter the folder name and click the **Create** button. After creating the folder, double-click on it. You can upload already existing files by selecting **Create > Import Files**.

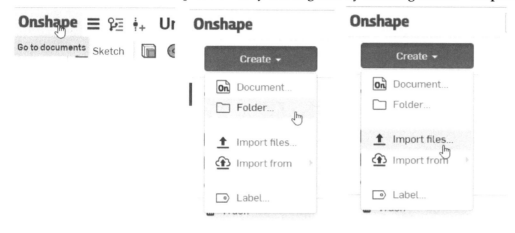

Chapter 2: Sketch Techniques

This chapter covers the methods and commands to create a sketch in the Sketch Environment. In Onshape, you create a rough sketch and then apply dimensions and constraints that define its shape and size. The dimensions define the length, size, and angle of a sketch element, whereas constraints define the constraints between the sketch elements.

Tutorial 1 (Millimetres)

In this example, you will draw the sketch shown below.

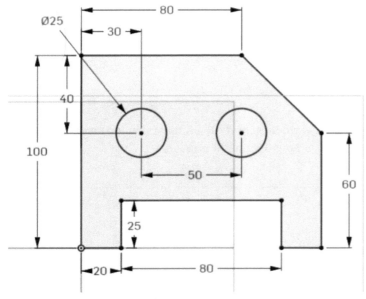

Creating a New document

1. In your Internet Browser, go to https://www.onshape.com to start Onshape.

2. Next, click **SIGN IN** button located on the top right corner side of the web page. Enter the username and password, and then, click **Sign in**.
3. On the Documents page, click **Create > Folder**. Next, type Chapter 2 in the **Folder name** box and then click **Create**.

4. Double-click on the **Chapter 2** folder in the Folders section; the folder appears.

5. On the Documents page, click **Create > Document**; the **New document** dialog appears on the screen.
6. Enter Tutorial 1 in the **Document name** box and click **OK**; a new document appears.

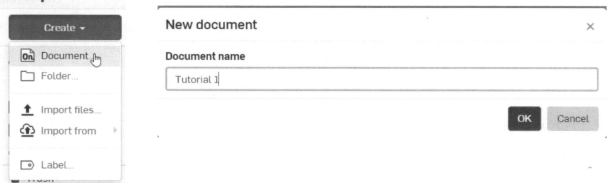

7. Click the **Document menu** located at the top left corner of the window and select **Workspace Units**; the **Workspace Units** dialog appears on the screen.
8. On the **Workspace Units** dialog, select **Default length unit > Millimeter** and **Default mass unit > Gram**.
9. Leave the other default settings and click the green check ✅.

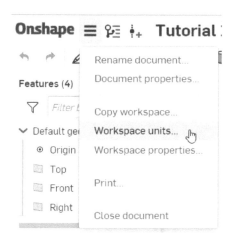

Creating a Sketch

1. To start a new sketch, click the **Sketch** command on the Toolbar.
2. Select on the Front plane.
3. Right-click and select **View normal to sketch plane**; the selected plane orients normal to the screen.

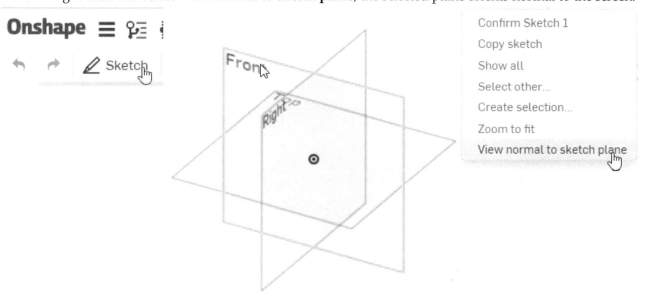

4. Activate the **Line** command (click the **Line** icon on the Toolbar).
5. Click on the origin point to define the first point of the line.
6. Move the pointer horizontally toward the right.
7. Click to define the endpoint of the line.
8. Move the pointer vertically upward, and then click to draw the second line.

9. Move the pointer horizontally toward the right and click.
10. Move the pointer vertically downward and click when the horizontal trace-lines appear from the sketch origin.
11. Move the pointer horizontally toward right up to a short distance, and then click.

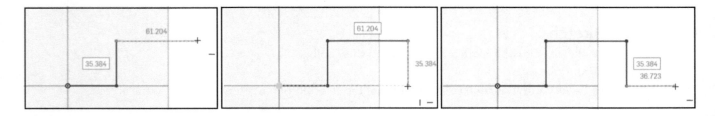

12. Move the pointer vertically upward and click.
13. Move the pointer in the top-left direction and click.
14. Move the pointer horizontally towards left and click when vertical trace-line appears from the origin.

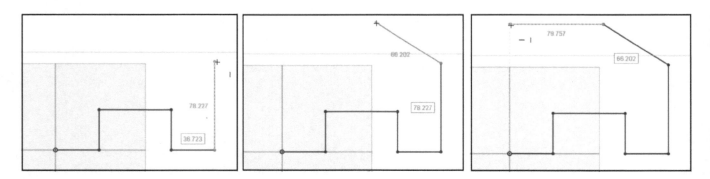

15. Select the start point of the sketch to create a closed sketch. Notice the shade inside the sketch.
16. Right-click and select **Escape Line** (or) press **Esc** to deactivate the **Line** command.

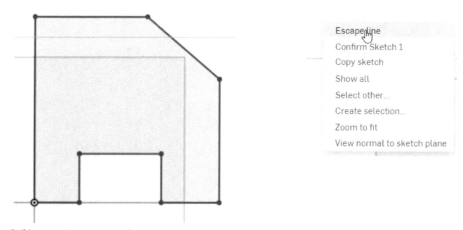

Adding Constraints

1. On the Toolbar, click **Constraint** drop-down > **Horizontal**.
2. Click on the two horizontal lines at the bottom.

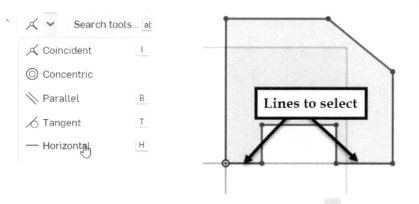

3. On the Toolbar, click **Constraint** drop-down > **Equal** = . Next, select the two horizontal lines at the bottom; the selected lines become equal in length.

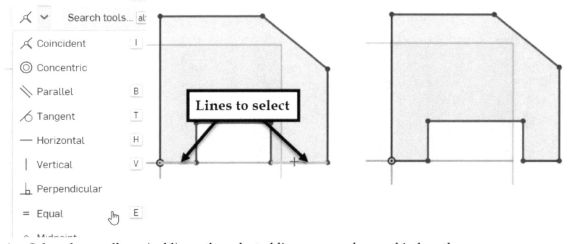

4. Select the small vertical lines; the selected lines are made equal in length.

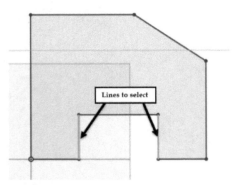

Adding Dimensions

1. Click **Dimension** ⟡ on the Toolbar and click on the lower left horizontal line. Move the mouse pointer downward and click to locate the dimension.
2. Type-in **20** and press Enter to update the dimension.

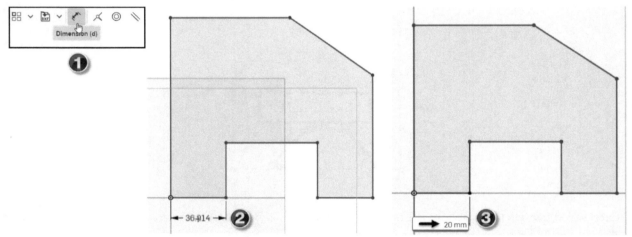

3. Click on the small vertical line located at the left side. Move the mouse pointer towards the right and click to position the dimension.
4. Type-in **25** and press Enter to update the dimension.

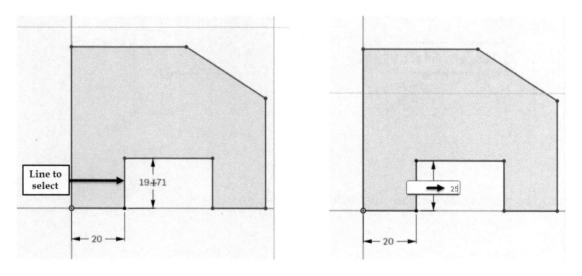

5. Create other dimensions in the sequence, shown below. Press Esc to deactivate the **Dimension** command.

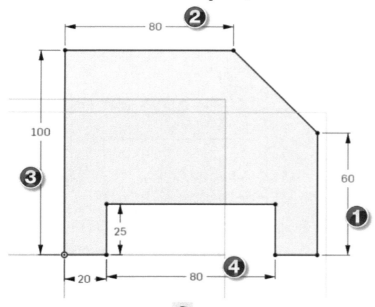

6. On the Toolbar, click **Circle** ⊙ . Click inside the sketch region to define the center point of the circle. Move the mouse pointer and click to define the diameter. Likewise, create another circle.

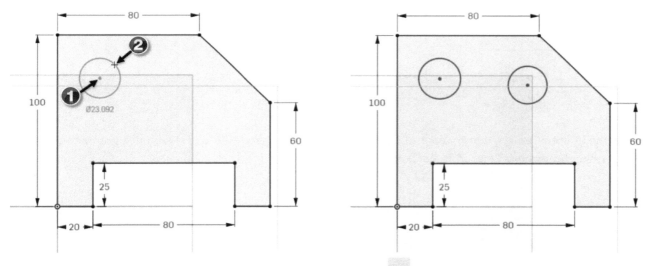

7. On the Toolbar, click **Constraints** drop-down > **Horizontal** ⎯ . Next, click on the center points of the two circles to make them horizontally aligned.

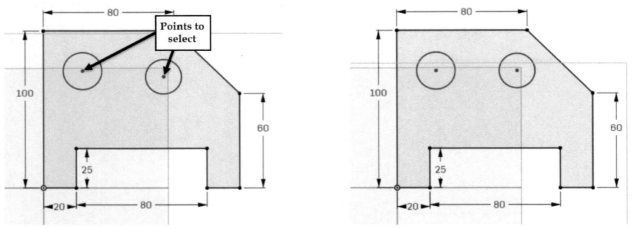

8. On the Toolbar, click **Constraints** drop-down > **Equal**. Next, click on the two circles; the diameters of the circles become equal.

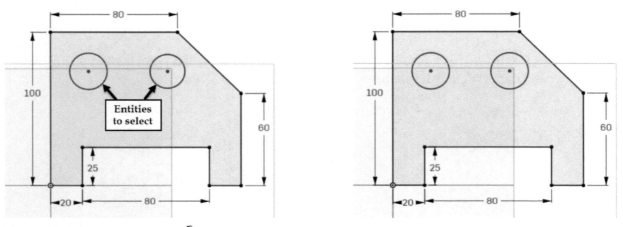

9. Activate the **Dimension** command and click on any one of the circles. Move the mouse pointer and click to position the dimension. Type **25** in the box and press Enter.

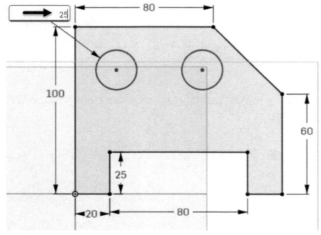

10. Create other dimensions between the circles and the adjacent lines, as shown below.

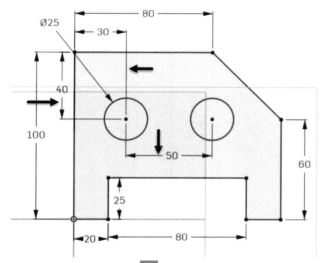

11. Click the green check  on the **Sketch 1** dialog or right-click and select **Confirm Sketch 1** to finish the sketch.

12. Click on the **Document menu** located at the top left corner and click **Close document**.

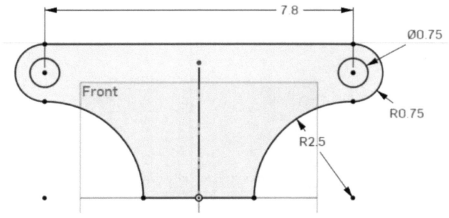

Tutorial 2 (Inches)

In this example, you draw the sketch shown below.

Creating a New document

1. To start **Onshape,** go to https://www.onshape.com.

2. Click the **SIGN IN** button located on the top right corner side of the window. Enter the username and password and then click **Sign in**.

3. On the Documents page, click **Create > Document**; the **New document** dialog appears on the screen.

4. On the Documents page, click **Create > Document**; the **New document** dialog appears on the screen.

5. Enter Tutorial 2 in the **Document name** box and click **OK**; a new document appears.

6. Click **Document menu** located at the top left corner of the window and select **Workspace Units**; the **Workspace Units** dialog appears on the screen.

7. On the **Workspace Units** dialog, select **Default length unit > Inch** and **Default mass unit > Pound**.

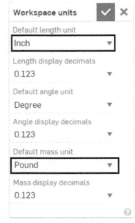

8. Leave the other default settings and click the green check ✓.

Creating a Sketch

1. To start a new sketch, click **Sketch** command on the Toolbar.

2. Click on the Front Plane.

3. Right-click and select **View normal to sketch plane**.

4. Click the **Line** ✏ command on the Toolbar.

5. Place the mouse pointer on the origin point and move the pointer horizontally toward the left; the dotted line appears. Click to specify the start point of a line.

6. Move the pointer horizontally towards the right and click to draw a line.

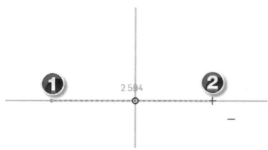

7. Right-click and click **Escape Line**.
8. Click **3 Point arc** on the Toolbar and click on the endpoint of the line.
9. Move the pointer vertically upward, and then move it in the top-right direction.
10. Click to define the endpoint of the arc.
11. Next, move the pointer and click to define the radius of the arc.

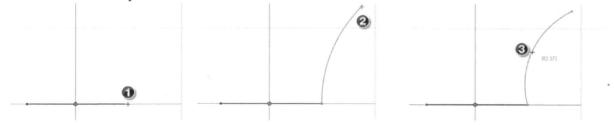

12. Press **Esc** to deactivate the **3 Point arc** command.

13. Click **3 Point arc** drop-down > **Tangent arc** on the Toolbar.

14. Click on the endpoint of the arc.

15. Place the pointer on the endpoint of the arc, and then move it upwards. Click when a vertical dotted line appears, as shown below.

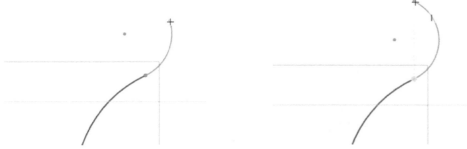

16. Next, right-click and click **Escape tangent arc** to deactivate the **Tangent arc** command.

17. Activate the **Line** command (click the **Line** icon on the Toolbar).

18. Move the mouse pointer towards left and click to create a horizontal line. Note that the length of the new line should be higher than that of the lower horizontal line.

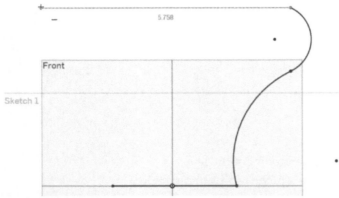

19. Press **Esc** to deactivate the **Line** command.

20. Activate the **Tangent arc** command and click on the endpoint of the line.

21. Move the pointer downwards left.

22. Move the pointer towards the right and click when a vertical dotted line appears, as shown below.

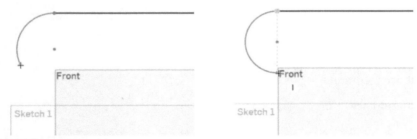

23. Press **Esc** to deactivate the tangent arc.

24. Activate the **3 Point arc** command and click on the endpoint of the tangent arc.

25. Select the start point of the sketch.

26. Move the pointer and click to define the radius of the arc.

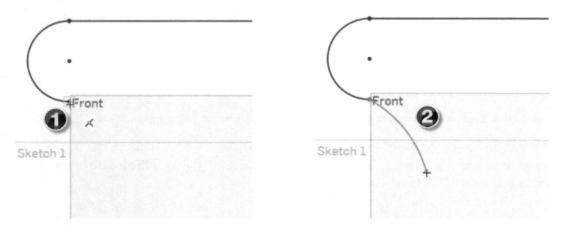

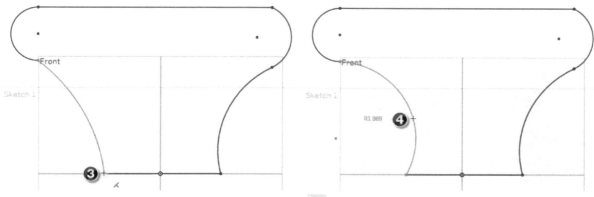

27. Activate the **Line** command (click the **Line** ✏ icon on the Toolbar).

28. Click on the origin point of the sketch. Move the mouse pointer vertically up and click to create a vertical line. Next, press Esc to deactivate the **Line** command.

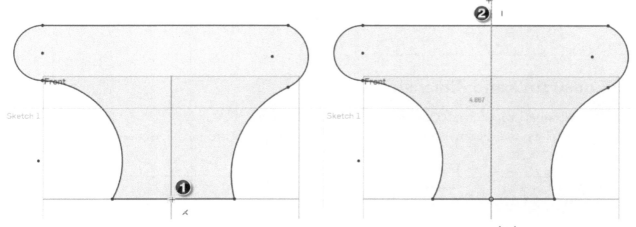

29. Click on the vertical line located at the center, and then click **Construction** ⇄ command on the Toolbar. The line turns into a construction element.

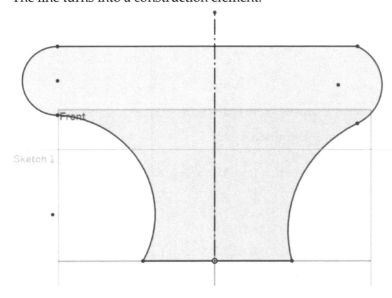

30. Activate the **Circle** 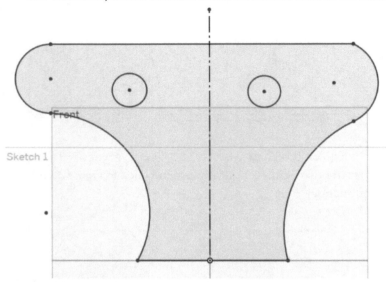 command. Click on the right side of the construction line to specify the center point. Move the pointer outward and click to create the circle.
31. Likewise, create another circle on the left side of the construction line.

Adding Constraints and dimensions

1. Click **Constraints** drop-down > **Concentric** on the Toolbar.
2. Click on the circle and the small arc on the right side. The circle and arc are made concentric.

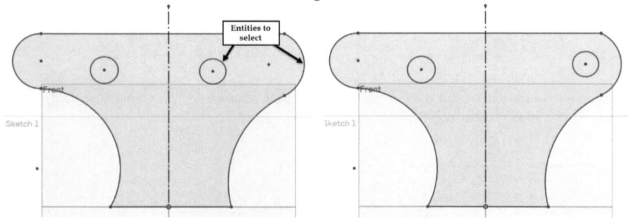

3. Likewise, make the other circle and small arc concentric to each other.
4. On the Toolbar, click **Constraints** drop-down > **Symmetric**.
5. Click on the construction line located at the center.
6. Click on the small arcs on both sides of the construction line. The arcs are made symmetric about the construction line.

24

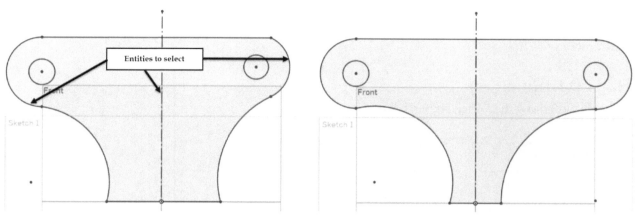

7. Likewise, make the large arcs and circles symmetric about the construction line.

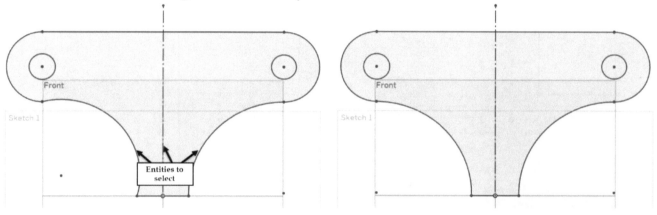

8. On the Toolbar, click **Constraints** drop-down > **Horizontal**. Next, select the center point of any one of the large arcs.
9. Select the origin point of the sketch; the two selected points are aligned horizontally.
10. Activate the **Dimension** command and apply dimensions to the sketch, as shown below.

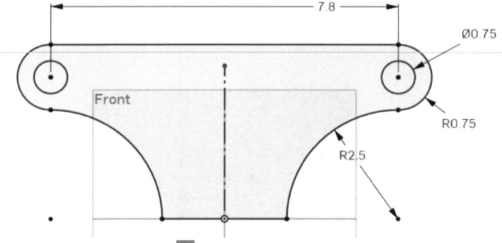

11. Click the green check ✔ on the **Sketch 1** dialog to exit the sketch.

12. To close the file, click **Document menu** ☰ located at the top left corner of the window and click **Close document**.

Tutorial 3 (Millimetres)

In this example, you draw the sketch shown below.

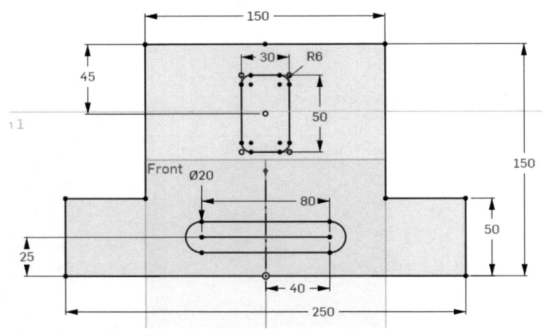

Creating a New Document

1. On the Documents page, click **Create > Document**; the **New document** dialog appears on the screen.

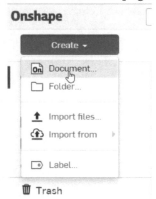

2. Enter Tutorial 3 in the **Document name** box and click **OK**; a new document appears.
3. Click **Document menu** located at the top left corner of the window and select **Workspace Units**; the **Workspace Units** dialog appears on the screen.
4. On the **Workspace Units** dialog, select **Default length unit > Millimeter** and **Default mass unit > Gram**.
5. Leave the other default settings as it is and click green check ✓ on the **Workspace Units** dialog.

Creating a Sketch

1. To start a new sketch, click **Sketch** command on the Toolbar.
2. Click on the Front plane.
3. Right-click and select **View normal to sketch plane**; the selected plane orients normal to the screen.
4. Activate the **Line** command (click the **Line** icon on the Toolbar).
5. Click on the origin point and move the pointer vertically up. Next, click to create a vertical line.

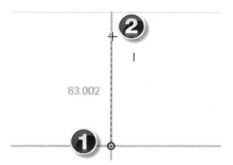

6. Press **Esc** to deactivate the line command.
7. Select the vertical line and click the **Construction** command. It creates a vertical centerline.

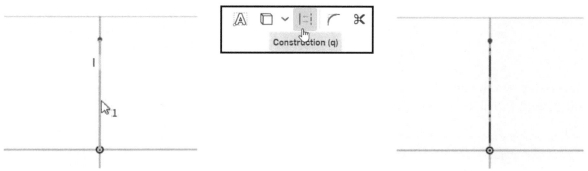

8. Activate the **Line** command and click on the origin point.
9. Move the mouse pointer horizontally towards the right and click to define the second point.
10. Draw the lines in the sequence, as shown. Next, right-click in the graphics area and select **Escape line**.

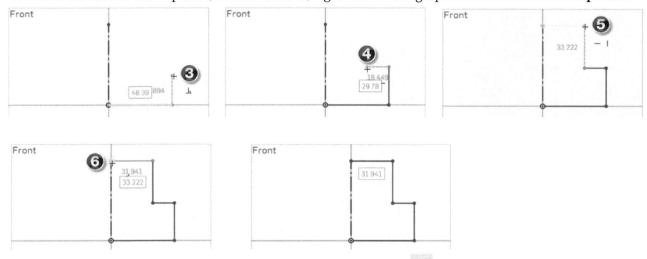

11. Activate the **Mirror** command (On the Toolbar, click the **Mirror**).

27

12. Select the vertical centreline to define the mirror line.
13. Select the entities to mirror, as shown.

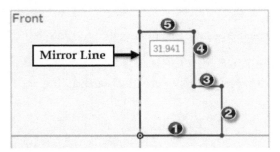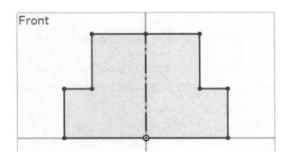

14. Press **Esc** to deactivate the **Mirror** command.
15. On the **Sketch 1** dialog, check the **Show constraints** option to view all the constraints.

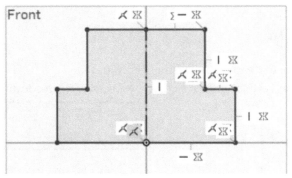

You can notice the symmetric constraints on both sides of the mirror line.

16. On the **Sketch 1** dialog, uncheck the **Show constraints** option to hide the constraints.

17. Click **Rectangle** drop-down **> Center point rectangle** on the Toolbar.
18. Click on the centreline to define the center of the rectangle.
19. Move the mouse pointer towards top right corner and click to define the corner of the rectangle.

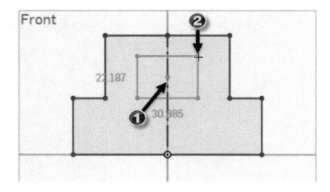

20. Click the **Line** command on the Toolbar.
21. Specify the start and endpoints of the line, as shown.

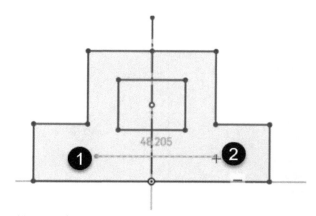

22. On the Toolbar, click **Offset** drop-down > **Slot** and select the horizontal line, as shown.

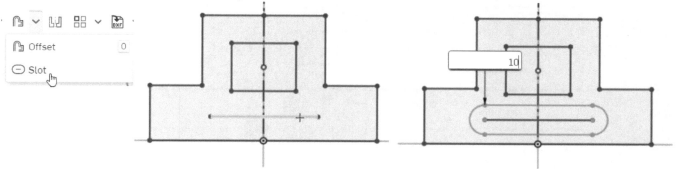

23. Double click on the dimension value attached to the slot, and then enter 10. Next, press Esc to deactivate the **Slot** command.
24. Click the **Sketch Fillet** command on the Toolbar.
25. Select the corners of the rectangle and click to create the fillet, as shown.
26. Double click on the fillet radius value and type-in 6 in the box. Then, press **Enter** to update the radius value.

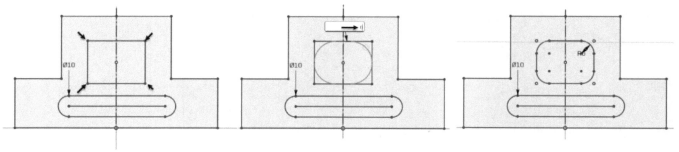

27. Activate the **Dimension** command and apply dimensions in the sequence shown below.

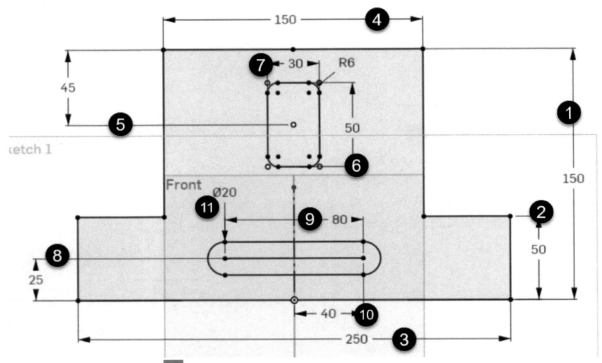

28. Click the green check ✓ on the **Sketch 1** dialog to finish the sketch.
29. Click on the **Document menu** located at the top left corner of the window and click **Close document** to close.

Exercises

Exercise 1

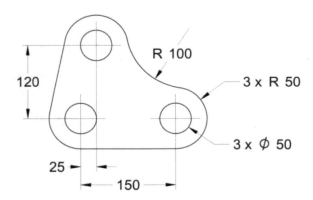

Exercise 2

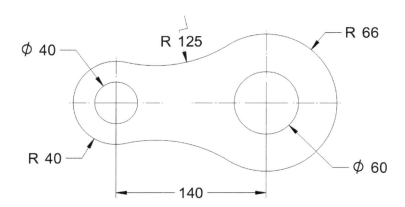

Exercise 3

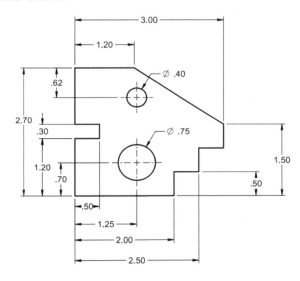

Chapter 3: Extrude and Revolve Features

This chapter covers the methods and commands to create extruded and revolved features.

Tutorial 1 (Millimeters)

In this example, you create the part shown below.

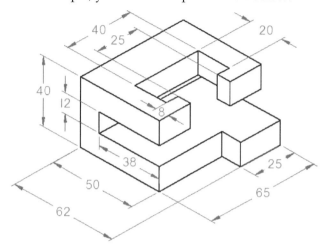

Creating a New Document

1. In your Internet Browser, go to https://www.onshape.com to start Onshape.

2. Next, click **SIGN IN** button located on the top right corner side of the web page. Enter the username and password, and then, click **Sign in**.
3. On the Documents page, click **Create > Folder**. Next, type Chapter 3 in the **Folder name** box and then click **Create**.
4. Double-click on the **Chapter 3** folder in the Folders section; the folder appears.
5. On the Documents page, click **Create > Document**; the **New document** dialog appears on the screen.
6. Enter Tutorial 1 in the **Document name** box and click **OK**; a new document appears.
7. Click the **Document menu** located at the top left corner of the window and select **Workspace Units**; the **Workspace Units** dialog appears on the screen.
8. On the **Workspace Units** dialog, select **Default length unit > Millimeter** and **Default mass unit > Gram**.
9. Leave the other default settings and click the green check ✅.

Creating a Sketch

1. To start a new sketch, click **Sketch** command on the Toolbar.

2. Click on the Front plane. Next, right-click and select **View normal to sketch plane**; the selected plane orients normal to the screen.
3. On the Toolbar, click **Rectangle** drop-down > **Corner rectangle**□. Next, click the origin point to define the first corner of the rectangle.
4. Move the pointer toward the top right and click to define the second corner.
5. Activate the **Dimension** (on the Toolbar, click the **Dimension** command).
6. Select the horizontal line, move the pointer upward, and click. Next, type in 50 in the box and press Enter.
7. Likewise, apply a dimension of 40 mm to the vertical line. On the **Sketch 1** dialog, click the green check.

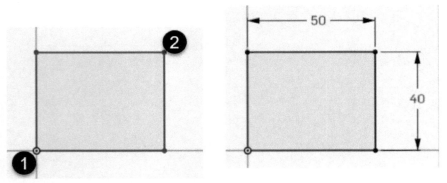

Creating an Extruded Feature

1. On the Toolbar, click the **Extrude** command. Next, click on the region enclosed by the sketch.
2. On the **Extrude** dialog, click **End Type > Symmetric**. On the **Extrude** dialog, type-in **65** in the **Depth** box.
3. Click the green check to complete the *Extrude* feature.

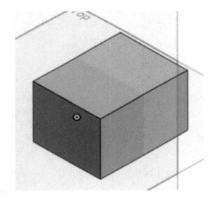

Creating an Extruded Cut Feature

1. Click the **Sketch** command on the Toolbar. Next, click on the front face of the part geometry.
2. To change the view orientation normal to the sketch plane, right-click and select **View normal to sketch plane**.
3. On the Toolbar, click the **Corner rectangle** □ command.
4. Click on the right edge of the model, move the pointer toward left, and then click.

5. Activate the **Dimension** ⟋ command and then select the horizontal line of the rectangle. Next, move the pointer upward, and then click to position the dimension. Type **38** in the box, and then press Enter to update the dimension.

6. Select the bottom edge of the model and the lower horizontal line of the rectangle. Move the pointer toward the right and click to position the dimension — type **14** in the box, and then press Enter.

7. Likewise, apply the remaining dimension to the sketch.

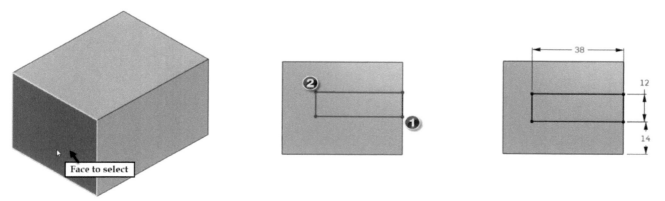

8. On the **Sketch 2** dialog, click green check ✓ to confirm the sketch.

9. Click the **Extrude** 🗔 command on the Toolbar; the **Extrude** dialog pops-up on the screen.

10. Click the **Remove** tab on the **Extrude** dialog. Next, select the sketch from the graphics area.

11. On the **Extrude** dialog, select **End Type > Through All**.

12. Click the green check ✓ on the **Extrude** dialog to create the cut throughout the part geometry.

13. Click the **Camera and render options** drop-down located at the right-side in the graphics area.

14. Select the **Isometric** option to change the view orientation to the isometric view.

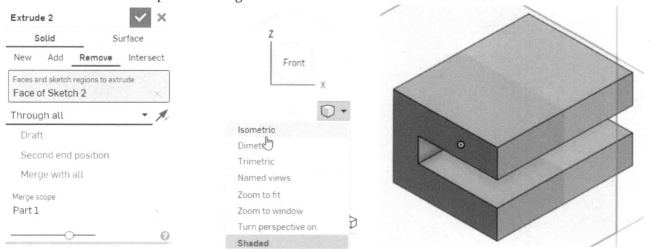

Extruding a sketch Up to the Face next to the sketch plane

1. Click the **Sketch** command on the Toolbar and click on the top face of the part geometry.

2. Click the right mouse button and select **View normal to sketch plane** to change the view orientation normal to the sketch plane.

3. Activate the **Line** command (click the **Line** ✏️ icon on the Toolbar).
4. Select the origin point of the sketch, move the pointer towards the right and click.
5. Press **Esc** to deactivate the **Line** command.
6. Select the line from the part geometry and click the **Construction** command on the Toolbar.

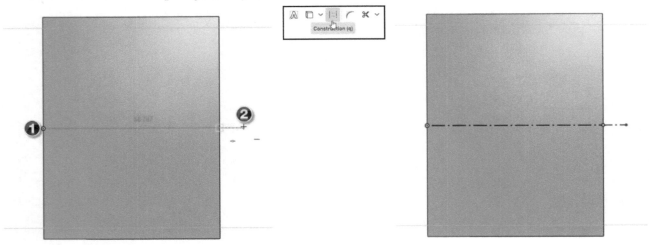

7. Activate the **Line** command and click on the intersection point between the construction line and right model edge.
8. Create the sketch, as shown.

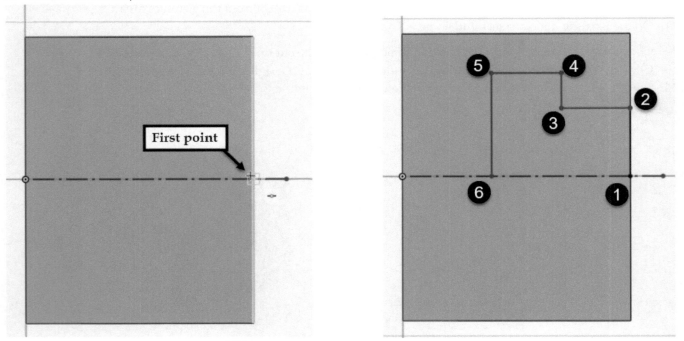

9. On the Toolbar, click the **Mirror** command and select the construction line from the part geometry as the mirror line.
10. Select the other entities to mirror them, as shown. Right click and select Escape mirror.

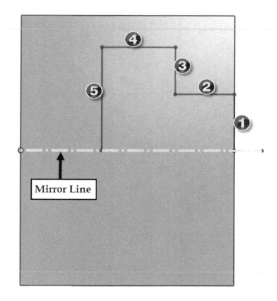 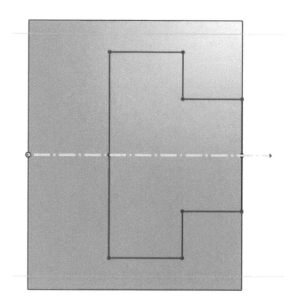

11. Click the **Dimension** [✐] command on the Toolbar.
12. Add dimensions to the sketch, as shown.

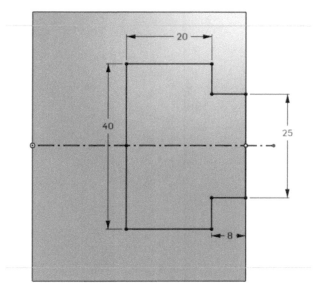

13. Click the green check ✅ on the **Sketch 3** dialog to confirm the sketch.
14. Change the view orientation to Isometric by clicking the **Camera and render options** drop-down **> Isometric** located at the right side of the graphics area.
15. Activate the **Extrude** 🗗 command and select the sketch.
16. Click the **Remove** tab and select **End Type > Up to next** from the **Extrude** dialog.
17. Click the green check ✅ to remove the material up to the surface next to the sketch plane.

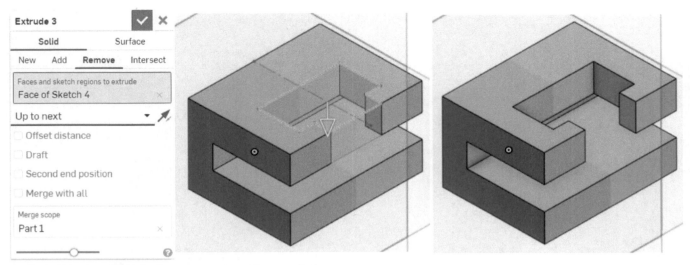

Extruding a sketch up to a selected face

1. Activate the **Sketch** command and select the Top plane.
2. Draw a closed sketch and apply dimensions to it, as shown.
3. On the Toolbar, click **Constraints** drop-down > **Coincident**. Next select the corner point of the rectangle and the model, as shown.
4. Click the green check on the **Sketch 4** dialog to confirm the sketch.

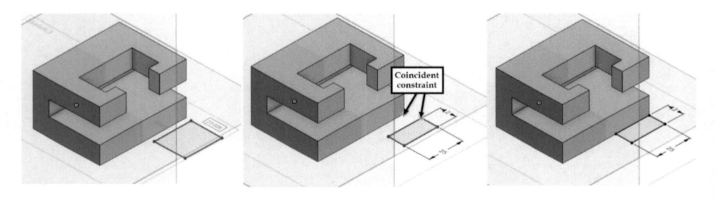

5. Activate the **Extrude** command and select the sketch
6. Select **End type > Up to face** from the **Extrude** dialog. Next, select the horizontal face of the part geometry, as shown.
7. Click the green check on the **Extrude** dialog to complete the part.

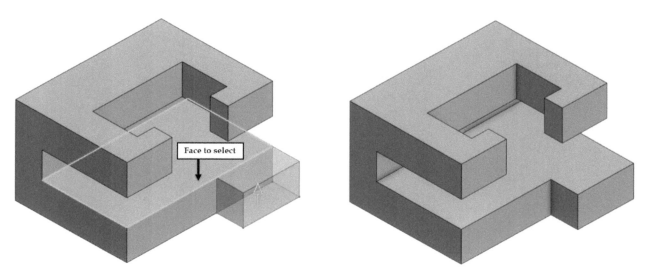

8. Click on the **Document menu** located at the top-left corner of the window, and then select **Close document** to close the document.

Tutorial 2 (Inches)

In this example, you create the part shown below.

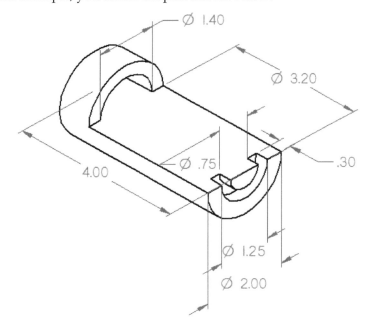

Creating a New document

1. On the Documents page, click **Create > Document**; the **New document** dialog appears on the screen.

2. Enter Tutorial 3 in the **Document name** box and click **OK**; a new document appears.
3. Click **Document menu** located at the top left corner of the window and select **Workspace Units**; the **Workspace Units** dialog appears on the screen.
4. On the **Workspace Units** dialog, select **Default length unit > Inches** and **Default mass unit > Pound**.
5. Leave the other default settings as it is and click the green check ✅ on the **Workspace Units** dialog.

Creating a Revolved Feature

1. Click the **Sketch** command on the Toolbar.
2. Select the Top plane and change the view orientation to normal to the sketch plane.
3. On the Toolbar, click the **Corner rectangle** ▢ command.
4. Click the origin point to define the first corner of the rectangle.
5. Move the pointer toward the top right corner and click to define the second corner.
6. Add dimensions to the sketch, as shown. Click the green check ✅ on the **Sketch1** dialog to confirm the sketch.

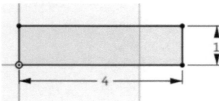

7. On the Toolbar, click the **Revolve** ⟳ command.
8. Select the sketch and click on the line, as shown.

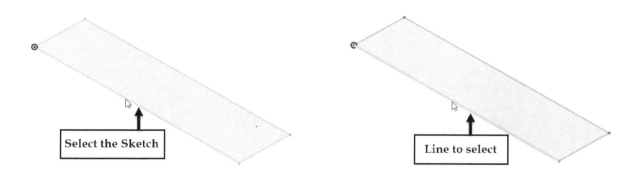

9. On the **Revolve** dialog, click the **Revolve type** drop-down **> One direction**.
10. Type-in 180 in the **Revolve Angle** field.
11. Click the **Opposite direction** ↻ button.
12. Click the green check ✓ to create the *Revolved* feature.

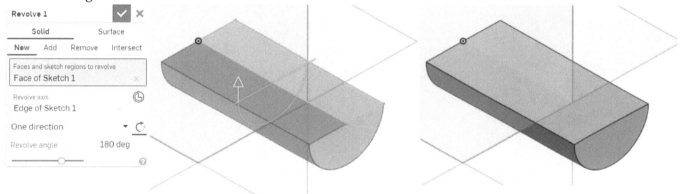

Creating a Revolved Cut feature

1. Click the **Sketch** command on the Toolbar and select the top face of the part geometry.

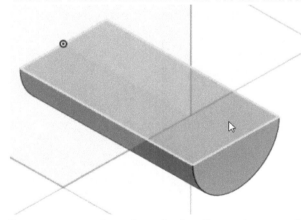

2. Draw a rectangle and apply the dimensions, as shown. In addition to that, draw a horizontal construction line passing through the origin.

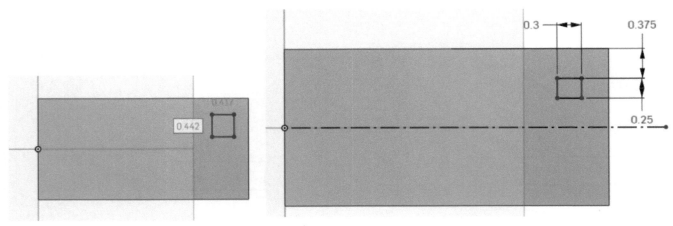

3. Click **Constraints** drop-down > **Coincident** ⚞ on the toolbar and select the left vertical line of the rectangle. Next, select the left vertical edge of the model. Click the green check on the **Sketch 2** dialog.

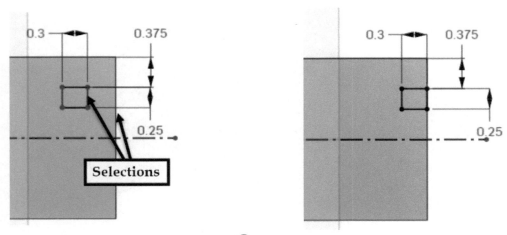

4. On the Toolbar, click the **Revolve** ◓ icon and click the **Remove** tab on the **Revolve** dialog.
5. Click on the region enclosed by the rectangle.
6. Click on the **Revolve axis** selection box, and then select the construction line from the part geometry.
7. Click the green check ✓ to create the revolved cut.

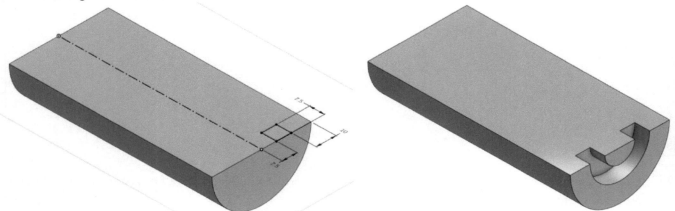

Adding a Revolved Feature to the Model

1. Activate the **Sketch** command and click on the top face of the part geometry.
2. Draw the sketch and apply dimensions and constraint, as shown. Create a horizontal construction line passing through the origin. Click the green check on the **Sketch 3** dialog.

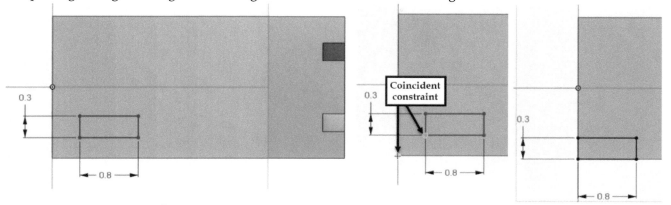

3. Activate the **Revolve** command and select the sketch.
4. On the **Revolve** dialog, click **Revolve axis** and select the construction line from the part geometry.
5. Click the **Revolve type** drop-down > **One direction** and type-in **180** in the **Revolve angle** box.
6. Click the **Opposite direction** button.
7. Click **green check** to add the *Revolved* feature to the geometry.

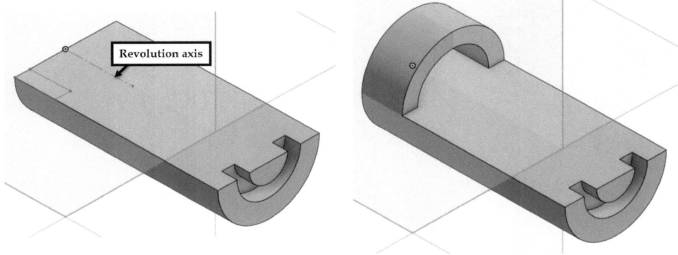

8. Click **Document menu** located at the top-left corner of the window and click the **Close document** option to close the file.

Exercises
Exercise 1

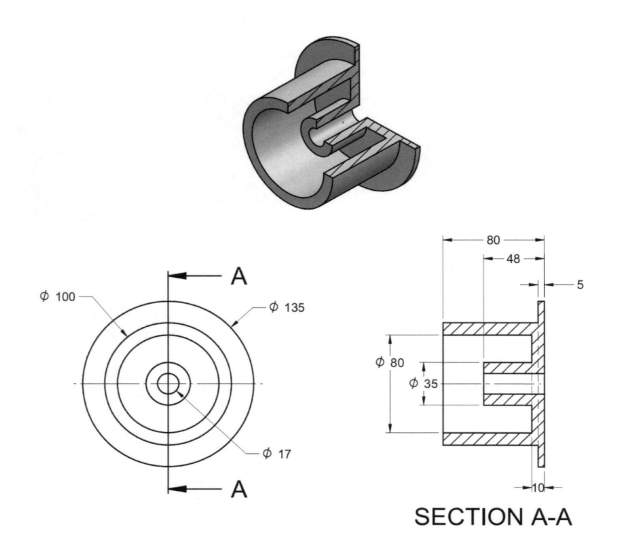

Exercise 2

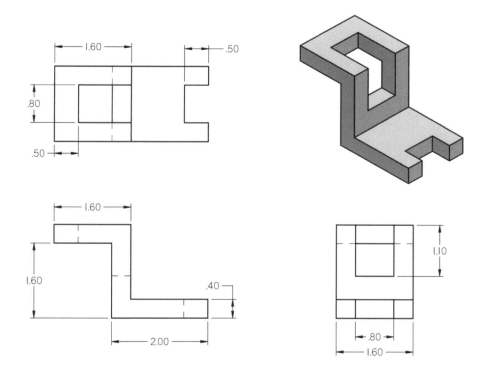

Exercise 3

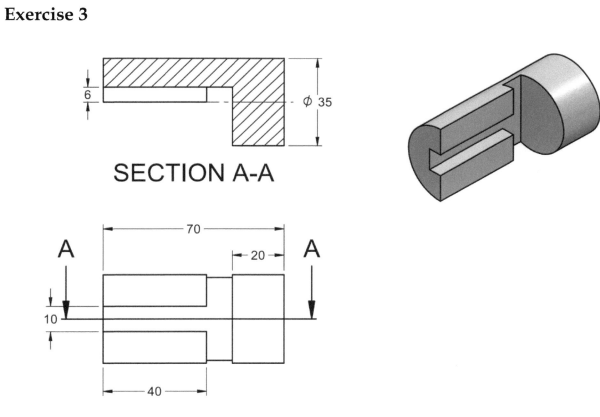

SECTION A-A

Chapter 4: Placed Features

So far, all of the features covered in the previous chapter are based on two-dimensional sketches. However, there are certain features in ONSHAPE that do not require a sketch at all. Features that do not require a sketch are called Placed features. You can simply place them on your models. However, you must have some existing geometry to add these features. Unlike a sketch-based feature, you cannot use a Placed feature for the first feature of a model. For example, to create a *Fillet* feature, you must have an already existing edge. In this chapter, you learn how to add Holes and Placed features to your design.

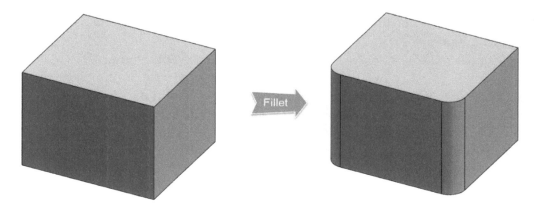

Tutorial 1 (Millimetres)

In this example, you create the part shown below.

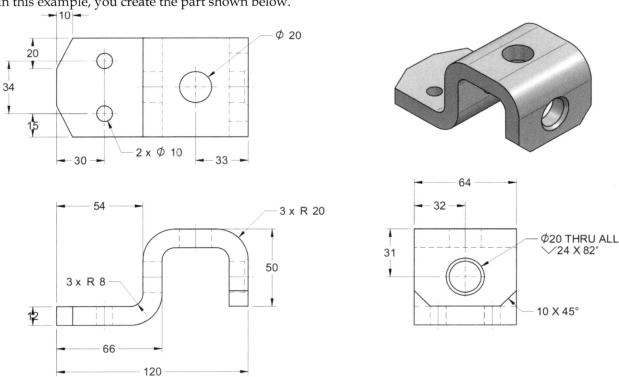

Creating a New document

1. In your Internet Browser, go to https://www.onshape.com to start Onshape.

2. Next, click **SIGN IN** button located on the top right corner side of the web page. Enter the username and password, and then, click **Sign in**.
3. On the Documents page, click **Create > Folder**. Next, type Chapter 4 in the **Folder name** box and then click **Create**.
4. Double-click on the **Chapter 4** folder in the **Folders** section.
5. On the Documents page, click **Create > Document**; the **New document** dialog appears on the screen.
6. Enter Tutorial 1 in the **Document name** box and click **OK**; a new document appears.
7. Click the **Document menu** located at the top left corner of the window and select **Workspace Units**; the **Workspace Units** dialog appears on the screen.
8. On the **Workspace Units** dialog, select **Default length unit > Millimeter** and **Default mass unit > Gram**.
9. Leave the other default settings and click the green check ✅.

Creating the Extruded Feature

1. Click **Sketch** command on the Toolbar. Next, click on the Front plane.
2. Right-click and select **View normal to sketch plane**; the selected plane orients normal to the screen.
3. Activate the **Line** command and create the sketch, as shown.
4. On the Toolbar, click the **Offset** command and select all the lines of the sketch. Next, click the arrow such that it points in the upward direction.

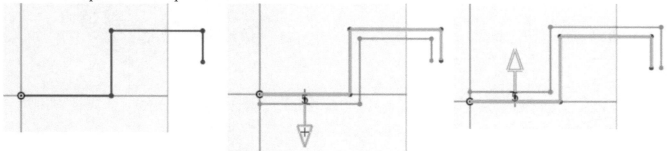

5. Click on the graphics area, and then type 12 in the offset distance box. Next, press Enter.
6. Close the ends of the sketch using the **Line** command.

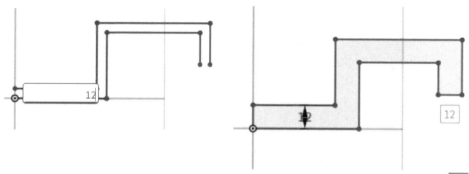

7. Add dimensions to constrain the sketch fully. Click the green check ✅ on the **Sketch 1** dialog.

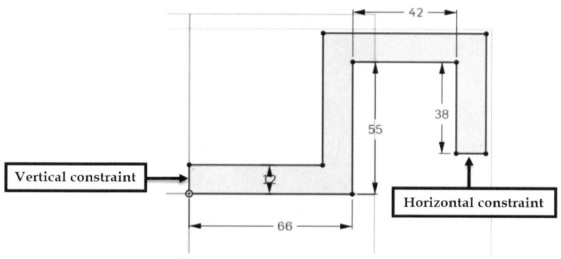

8. Activate the **Extrude** 🗔 command, and then select the sketch.
9. On the **Extrude** Dialog, select **End type > Symmetric**.

10. Type **64** in the **Depth** box and click the green check ✅ icon on the dialog.

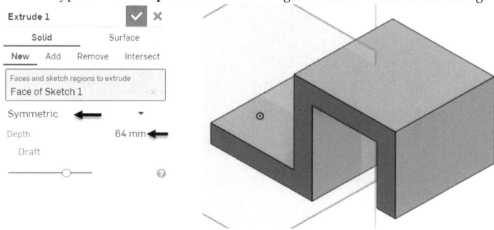

Creating the Hole Features

1. Click the **Sketch** command on the Toolbar, and then click on the right-side face.

2. On the Toolbar, click the **Point** ° command and then click on the sketch plane.

3. Apply the dimension between the point and the adjacent edges, as shown. Click the green check on the **Sketch 2** dialog.

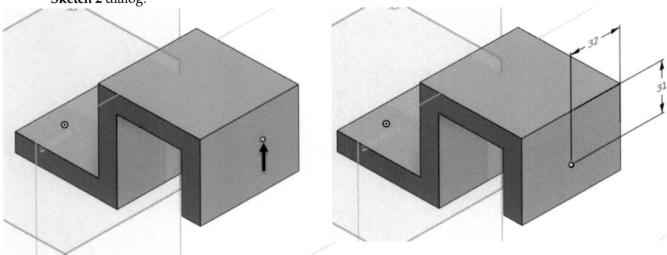

4. On the Toolbar, click the **Hole** command.
5. On the **Hole** dialog, click **Style > Countersink**.
6. Select **Termination > Through**.
7. Select **Standard > ISO** and **Hole Type > Clearance**, respectively.
8. Select **Size > M20** and **Fit > Close**, respectively.
9. In the **Hole** section, select **Size > M20**, and then check the **Show custom sizing** option.
10. Type-in 24 and 82 in the **Countersink diameter** and **Countersink angle** boxes, respectively.
11. Select the sketch point, and then click the green check on the **Hole** dialog.

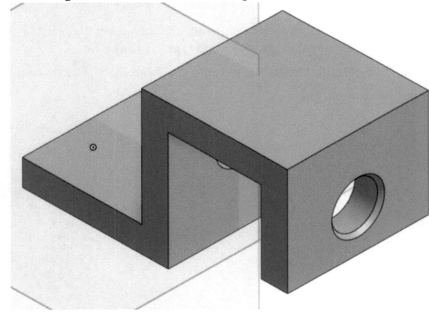

12. Click the **Sketch** command on the Toolbar, and then click on the top face.

13. On the Toolbar, click the **Point** ° command and then click on the sketch plane.
14. Apply the dimension between the point and the adjacent edges, as shown. Click the green check on the **Sketch 3** dialog.

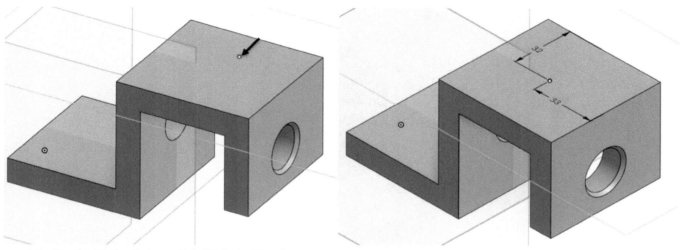

15. On the **Hole** dialog, click **Style > Simple**.
16. Select **Termination > Through**.
17. Type-in 20 in the **Diameter** box.
18. Select the sketch point, and then click the green check on the **Hole** dialog.

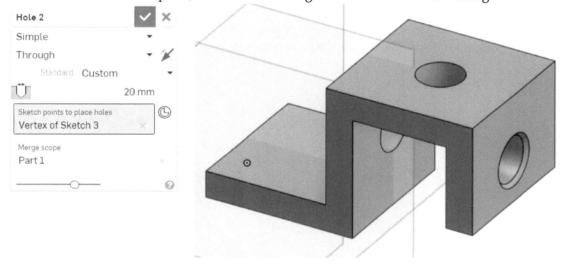

19. On the **View Cube**, click on the top left corner; the view orientation of the model changes.

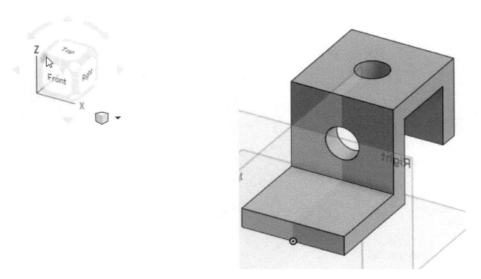

20. Click the **Sketch** command on the Toolbar, and then click on the lower top face of the model.

21. On the Toolbar, click the **Point** ° command and then click on the sketch plane.
22. Apply the dimension between the point and the adjacent edges, as shown.
23. On the Toolbar, click **Constraint** drop-down > **Vertical**. Next, select the two sketch points to align them vertically.
24. Click the green check on the **Sketch 4** dialog.

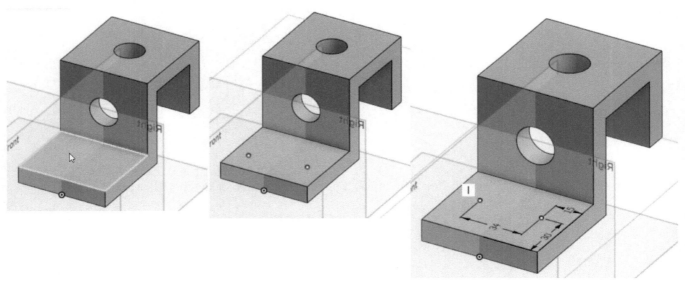

25. On the **Hole** dialog, click **Style > Simple**.
26. Select **Termination > Through**.
27. Type-in 20 in the **Diameter** box.

28. Select the sketch points, and then click the green check on the **Hole** dialog

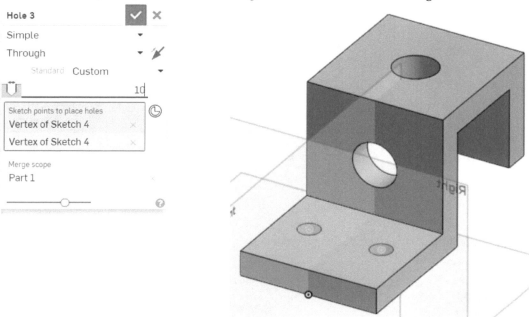

Creating Chamfers and Fillets

1. Click the **Chamfer** command on the Toolbar.
2. On the **Chamfer 1** dialog, select **Chamfer type > Two distances**.
3. Click on the vertical edges of the model, as shown.
4. Set the **Distance 1** and **Distance 2** to **10** and **20**, respectively. Click the green check on the dialog.

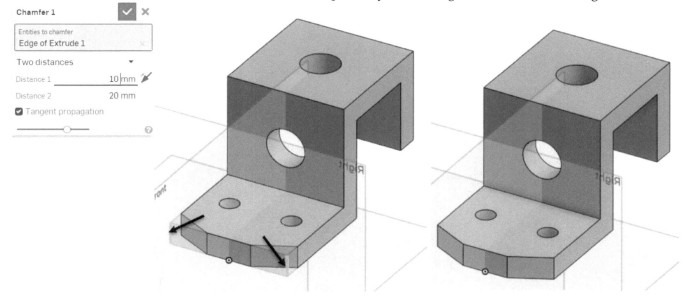

5. Click the **Fillet** command on the Toolbar.
6. On the **Fillet 1** dialog, select **Cross-section > Circular**.
7. Click on the horizontal edges of the geometry, as shown below (press and hold the right mouse button and drag to rotate the model).

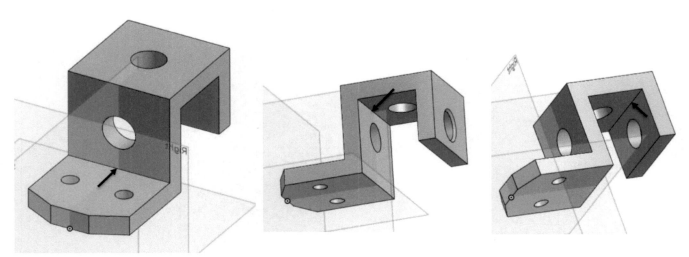

8. Type-in **8** in the **Radius** box, and then click the green check.

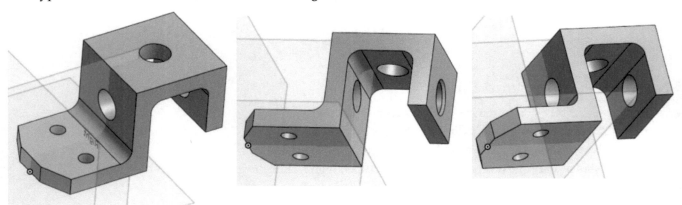

9. Activate the **Fillet** ⬜ command, and then click on the outer edges of the model, as shown below.

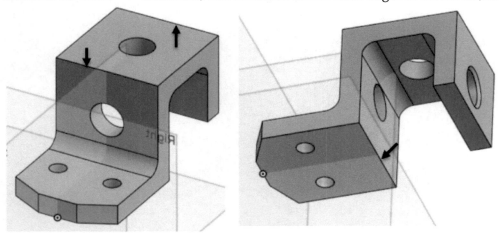

10. Type-in **20** in the Radius box. Click the green check to complete the fillet feature.

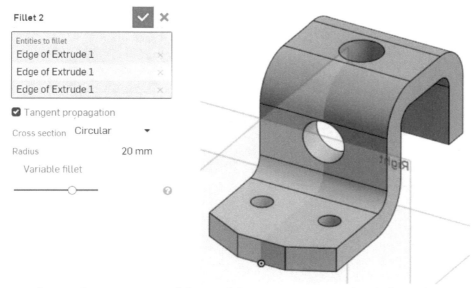

11. Change the orientation of the model view to Isometric by clicking the **Camera and Render options** drop-down, and selecting the **Isometric** option.

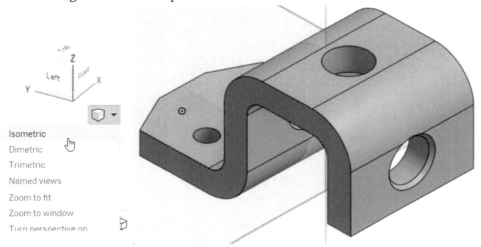

12. Click the **Chamfer** command on the Toolbar.
13. On the **Chamfer 1** dialog, select **Chamfer type > Distance and angle**.
14. Click on the lower corners of the part geometry.
15. Type-in **10** and 45 in the **Distance** and **Angle** boxes. Next, click the green check to chamfer the edges.

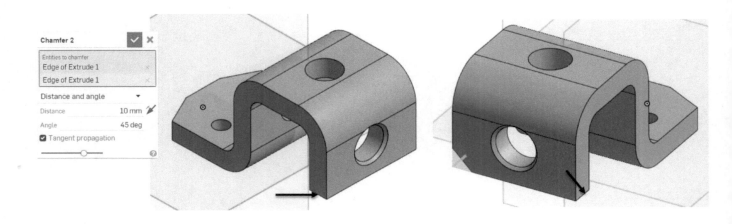

Exercises

Exercise 1 (Millimetres)

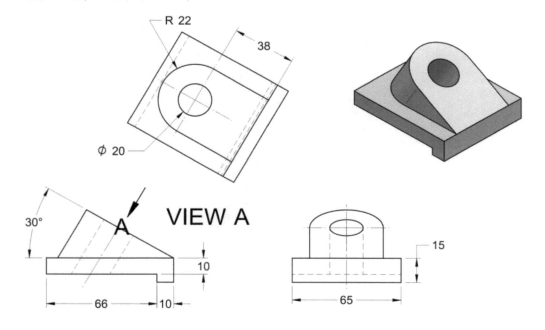

Exercise 2 (Inches)

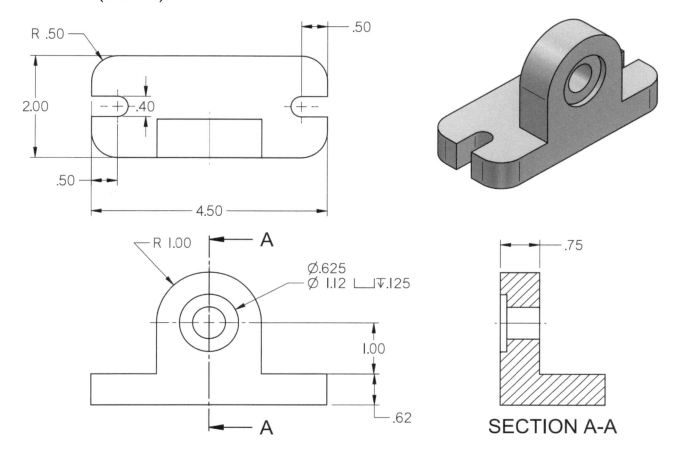

SECTION A-A

Chapter 5: Patterned Geometry

Tutorial 1

In this example, you create the part shown next.

.

.

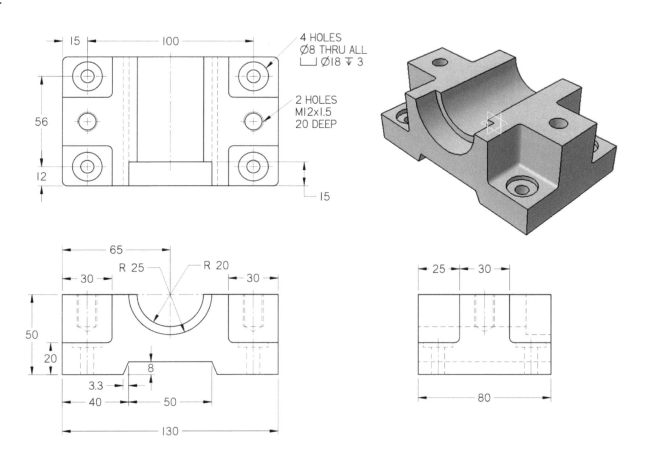

Creating a New document

1. In your Internet Browser, go to https://www.onshape.com to start Onshape.

2. Next, click **SIGN IN** button located on the top right corner side of the web page. Enter the username and password, and then, click **Sign in**.

3. On the Documents page, click **Create > Folder**. Next, type Chapter 5 in the **Folder name** box and then click **Create**.

4. Double-click on the **Chapter 5** folder in the Folders section.
5. On the Documents page, click **Create > Document**; the **New document** dialog appears on the screen.
6. Enter Tutorial 1 in the **Document name** box and click **OK**; a new document appears.
7. Click the **Document menu** located at the top left corner of the window and select **Workspace Units**; the **Workspace Units** dialog appears on the screen.
8. On the **Workspace Units** dialog, select **Default length unit > Millimeter** and **Default mass unit > Gram**.
9. Leave the other default settings and click the green check ☑.

Creating the Extruded features

1. To start a new sketch, click **Sketch** command on the Toolbar.
2. Click on the Front plane. Next, right-click and select **View normal to sketch plane**; the selected plane orients normal to the screen.
3. On the Toolbar, click **Rectangle** drop-down > **Center Point Rectangle** ⬚. Next, select the sketch origin and move the pointer outward.
4. Click to create a rectangle, and then apply dimensions to it. Next, click **green check** ☑ on the **Sketch 1** dialog.

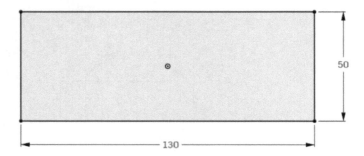

5. Activate the **Extrude** ⬚ command, and then select the sketch.
6. On the **Extrude** Dialog, click the **End type** drop-down > **Symmetric**.
7. Type **80** in the **Depth** box and click the green check ☑ on the dialog.
8. On the Toolbar, click the **Sketch** command. Next, click on the top face of the part geometry.
9. On the sketch Toolbar, click the **Rectangle** drop-down > **Corner Rectangle** ⬚.
10. Click on the corner point of the top face, as shown. Move the pointer in the top-left direction, and then click.
11. Add dimensions to the sketch.

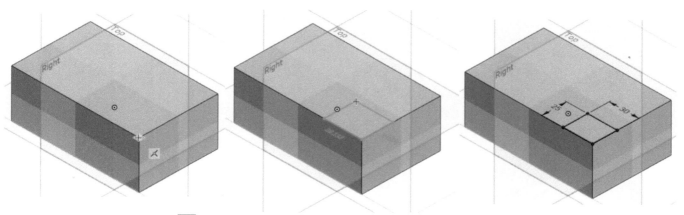

12. Click the green check ✔ on the **Sketch 2** dialog.

13. Activate the **Extrude** 🗐 command and click **Remove** tab on the **Extrude** dialog. Next, s30elect the sketch from the part geometry.

14. Type-in 30 in the **Depth** field.

15. Click the green check ✔ on the **Extrude** dialog.

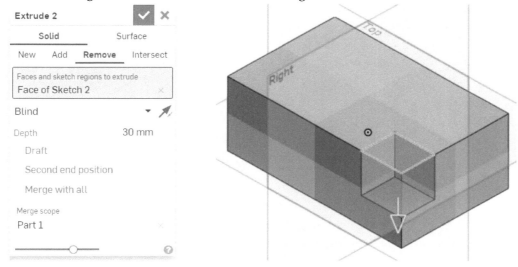

Creating the Hole features

1. On the Toolbar, click the **Sketch** command. Next, click on the bottom face of the **Extrude** cut feature, as shown.

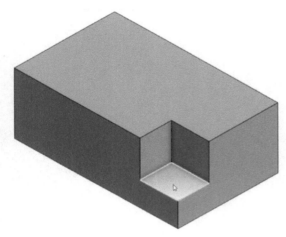

2. Create a sketch point on the bottom face of the Extrude feature. Next, add dimensions to the sketch, as shown.

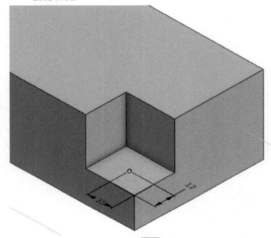

3. Click green check ✓ on the **Sketch 3** dialog.
4. Activate the **Hole** ◉ command. On the **Hole** dialog, select **Style > Counterbore**.
5. Select the sketch point on the part geometry. Next, select the **Termination** drop-down > **Through**.
6. Select the **Standard > Custom** option.
7. Set the hole **Diameter** value to **8**.
8. Type-in **18** and **3** in the **Counterbore diameter** and **Counterbore depth** fields, respectively; notice the preview of the counterbore hole on the part geometry.

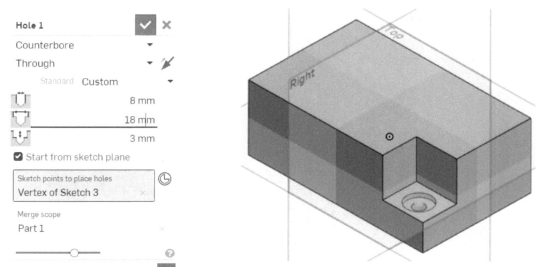

9. Click the green check ✅ on the **Hole** dialog to create the counterbore hole.
10. Click the **Sketch** command on the Toolbar. Next, click on the top face of the model.
11. On the sketch Toolbar, click the **Point** ° command. Next, place the point on the top face of the model.
12. Add dimensions to the sketch point, as shown.

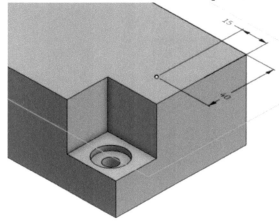

13. On the **Sketch 4** dialog, click the green check ✅ to confirm the sketch.
14. Activate the **Hole** command and select the sketch point. On the **Hole** dialog, click the **Style** drop-down **> Simple**.
15. Select **Standard > ISO** and **Hole type > Tapped**.
16. Select **Size > M12** and select **Pitch > 1.50 mm.**
Click the **Termination** drop-down **> Blind**.
17. Type **20** in the hole **Depth** and **Tapped Depth** fields respectively. Next, type **0** in the **Tap Clearance** field.
18. Click the green check ✅ on the **Hole** dialog to create the threaded hole.

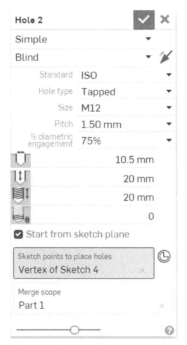

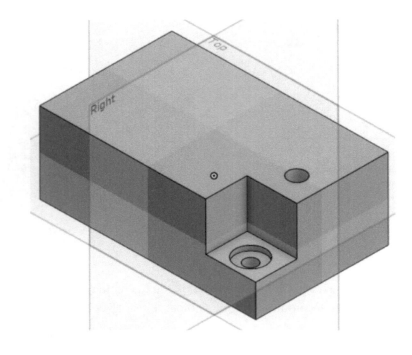

Creating the Linear pattern

1. On the Toolbar, click **Pattern** drop-down > **Linear pattern**.
2. On the **Linear pattern 1** dialog, click the **Pattern type** drop-down > **Feature pattern**.
3. Click the **Features to pattern** selection box.
4. Select the second *Extruded* feature and the *Counterbore Hole* from the part geometry.

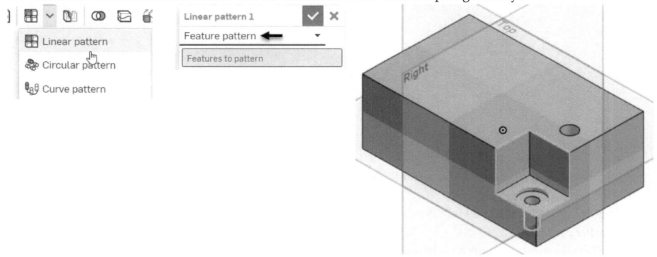

5. Next, click the **Direction** selection box and click on the top front edge of the part geometry.
6. Type-in **100** and **2** in the **Distance** and **Instance count** fields respectively.

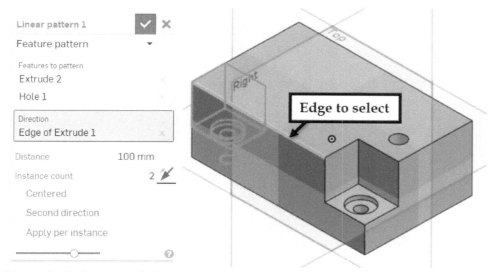

7. Next, check the **Second direction** option at the bottom of the dialog.
8. Click the **Direction** selection box and click on the top-right edge of the part geometry.

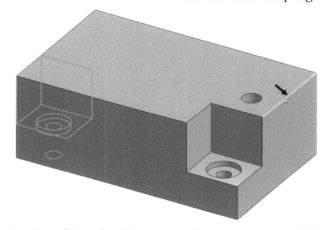

9. Type-in **55** and **2** in the **Distance** and **Instance count** fields, respectively.
10. Check the **Apply per Instance option** at the bottom of the dialog.
11. Click the green check ✓ on the **Linear pattern 1** dialog to pattern the features.

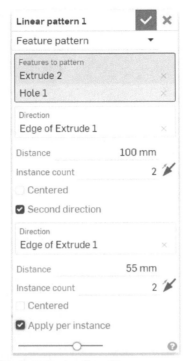

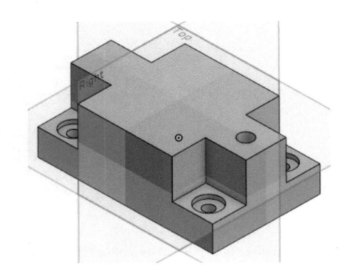

Mirroring the Features

1. On the Toolbar, click the **Mirror** command.
2. Click the **Mirror Type > Feature mirror** on the **Mirror** dialog.
3. Click the **Features to mirror** selection box and select the tapped hole.
4. Click the **Mirror plane** selection box and select the **Right** plane, as shown.

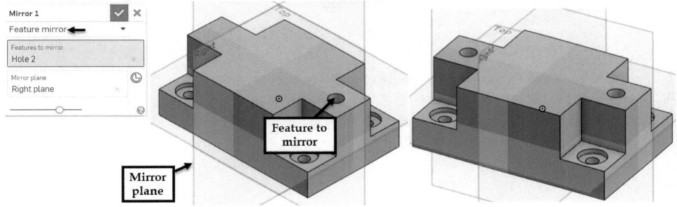

5. Click the green check on the **Mirror** dialog to mirror the selected features.

Creating the Hole and Extruded cut features

1. On the Toolbar, click the **Sketch** command and click on the front face of the part geometry.
2. Click the **Point** ° command on the toolbar. Next, click anywhere on the sketch plane.
3. On the Toolbar, click **Constraints** drop-down > **Midpoint**. Next, select the sketch point and the top front edge of the model; the point is constrained to the midpoint of the selected edge.

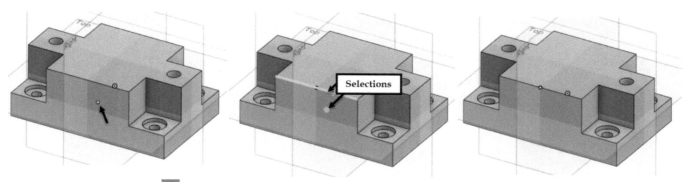

4. Click the green check ✔ on the **Sketch 5** dialog to confirm the sketch.
5. Activate the **Hole** command and select the sketch point.
6. On the **Hole** dialog, select the **Style > Counterbore**.
7. Select the **Termination > Through**.
8. Select the **Standard > Custom**.
9. Set the **Hole Diameter** value to **40**.
10. Type-in **50** and **15** in the **Counterbore diameter** and **Counterbore depth** fields, respectively.
11. Click the green check ✔ on the **Hole 3** dialog to create the counterbore hole.

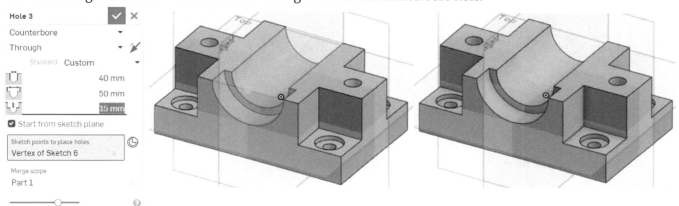

12. Sketch the front face of the part geometry and remove the material throughout the geometry using the **Extrude** command.

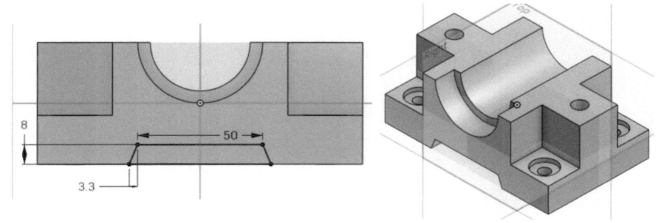

13. Activate the **Fillet** command and select the internal edges of the Extruded cut features, as shown.

14. Type **2** in the **Radius** box and click the green check.

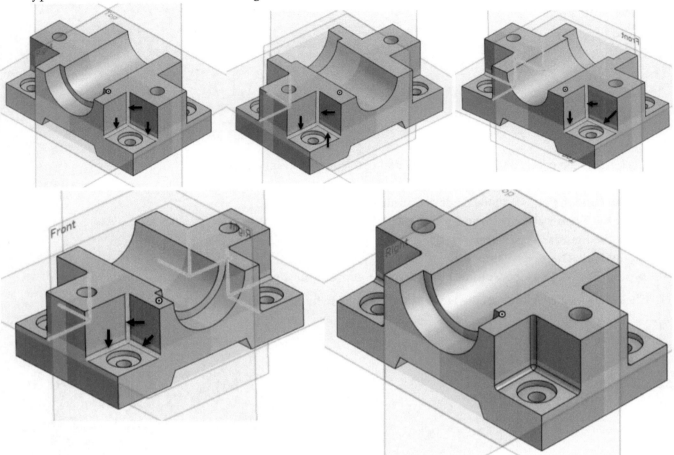

15. Click the **Document menu** located at the top-left corner of the graphics area and click the **Close document** option to close the document.

Exercises
Exercise 1

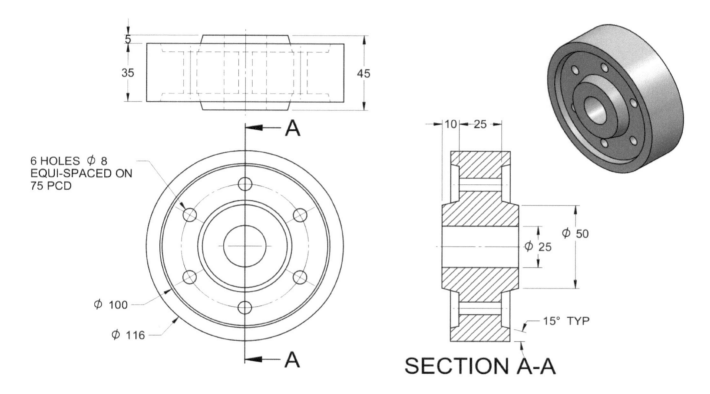

6 HOLES ϕ 8
EQUI-SPACED ON
75 PCD

ϕ 100

ϕ 116

5

35

45

A

A

10   25

ϕ 50

ϕ 25

15° TYP

SECTION A-A

Chapter 6: Sweep Features

Tutorial 1

In this example, you create the part shown below.

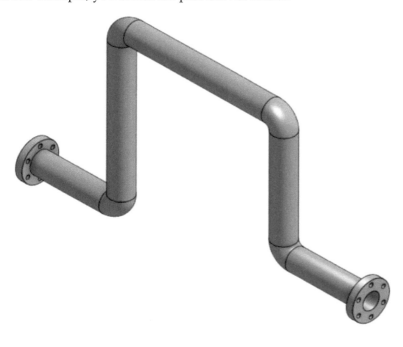

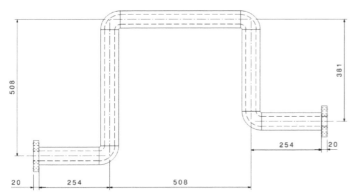

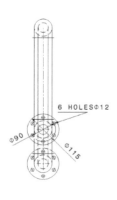

PIPE I.D. 51

PIPE O.D. 65

Creating a New document

1. In your Internet Browser, go to
   https://www.onshape.com to start
   Onshape.

2. Next, click **SIGN IN** button located on the top right corner side of the web page. Enter the username and password, and then, click **Sign in**.

3. On the Documents page, click **Create > Folder**. Next, type Chapter 6 in the **Folder name** box and then click **Create**.

4. Double-click on the **Chapter 6** folder in the **Folders** section.

5. On the Documents page, click **Create > Document**; the **New document** dialog appears on the screen.

6. Enter Tutorial 1 in the **Document name** box and click **OK**; a new document appears.

7. Click the **Document menu** located at the top left corner of the window and select **Workspace Units**; the **Workspace Units** dialog appears on the screen.

8. On the **Workspace Units** dialog, select **Default length unit > Millimeter** and **Default mass unit > Gram**.

9. Leave the other default settings and click the green check ✅.

Creating the Sweep Feature

1. To start a new sketch, click the **Sketch** command on the Toolbar.

2. Click on the Front plane.

3. Right-click and select **View normal to sketch plane**; the selected plane orients normal to the screen.

4. On the Toolbar, click the **Line** command and select the sketch origin.

5. Create the lines, as shown.

6. Right click and select Escape line.

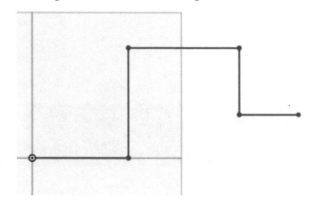

7. On the Toolbar, click the **Sketch fillet** command and select the corner points of the sketch.

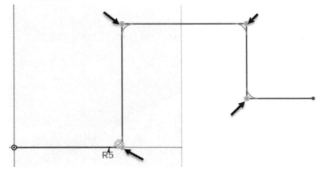

8. Click in the graphics area.

9. Type **38** and press Enter.

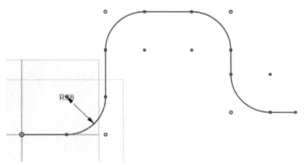

10. On the Toolbar, click the **Dimension** command.

11. Select the origin point and the vertical line.

12. Move the pointer downward and click to position the dimension.

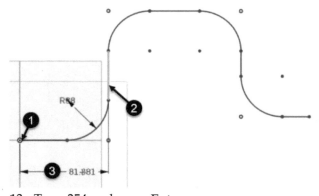

13. Type 254 and press Enter.

14. Select the two horizontal lines of the sketch.

15. Move the pointer toward the left and click to position the dimension.

16. Type 508 and press Enter.

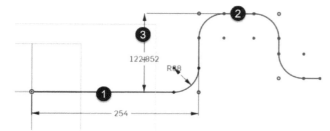

17. Likewise, apply the other dimensions to the sketch.

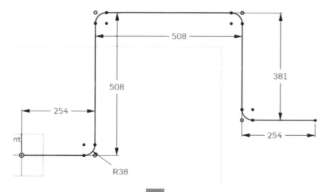

18. Click **green check** ✓ on the **Sketch 1** dialog.
19. Change the view orientation to Isometric view. (In the graphics area, click the **Camera and render options > Isometric** from the right-side).
20. On the Toolbar, click the **Plane** ⬜ command.
21. Click the **Plane type** drop-down > **Point normal**.

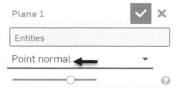

22. Select the lower horizontal line of the sketch to define the first entity.
23. Click on the end-point of the sketch to define the plane location.

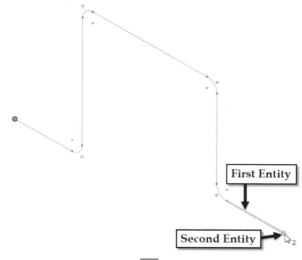

24. Click the green check ✓ on the **Plane** dialog to create a new plane.

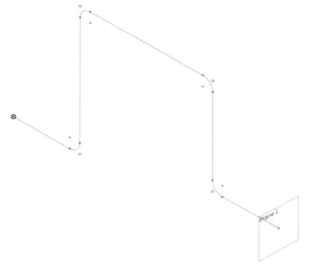

25. On the Toolbar, click the **Sketch** command.
26. Select the newly created plane.
27. On the Toolbar, click **Center point circle** command.
28. Specify the center point of the circle.
29. Move the pointer outward and click to create a circle.
30. Select the center point of the newly created circle.
31. Move the pointer outward and click to create another circle.

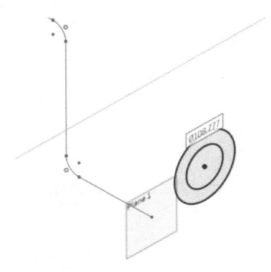

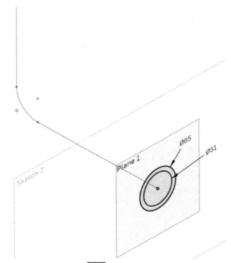

32. On the Toolbar, click Constraints drop-down > Coincident.
33. Select the center point of the circles.
34. Select the endpoint of the line.

40. Click the green check ☑ on the **Sketch 2** dialog.
41. On the Toolbar, click the **Sweep** 𝒫 command.
42. Zoom in to the circles, and then click on the region between the two circles.

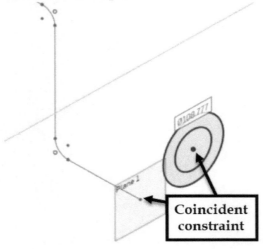

Coincident constraint

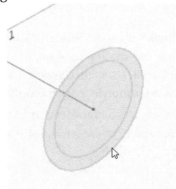

35. On the Toolbar, click the **Dimension** command.
36. Select the outer circle.
37. Type 65 and press Enter.
38. Select the other circle.
39. Type 51 and press Enter.

43. Click the **Sweep path** selection box and select the Sketch 1 from the **Features** window.

44. Click the green check 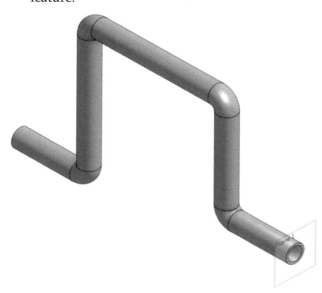 to create the *Sweep* feature.

Adding the Extruded Feature

1. Click the **Sketch** command on the Toolbar.
2. Click on the front-end face of the *Sweep* feature.

3. On the Toolbar, click the **Use (Project/Convert)** command.
4. Select the inner circular edge, as shown.

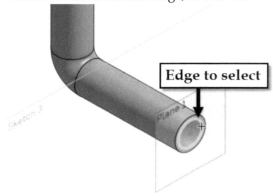

Edge to select

The edge is projected on to the sketch plane.

5. Draw a circle of 115 diameters.

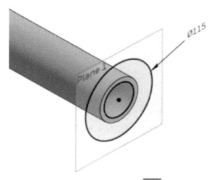

6. Click the green check on the **Sketch 3** dialog to confirm the sketch.
7. Activate the **Extrude** command.
8. Click on the regions enclosed by the sketch, as shown.

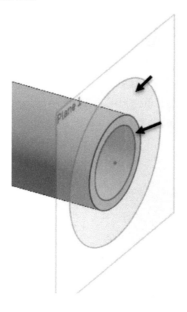

9. Type-in **20** in the **Depth** field. Click the **green** check ✓ to complete the *Extrude* feature.

Creating the Circular Pattern

1. Activate the **Sketch** command and select the face of the extruded feature, as shown.

2. On the Toolbar, click the **Point** command and click on the sketch plane.

3. Click the **Line** ✏ command on the Toolbar.
4. Click the **Construction** ⊟ command on the Toolbar.
5. Select centerpoint of the inner circular edge.

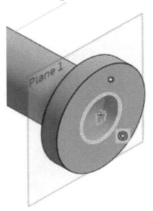

6. Move the pointer vertically upward and click.

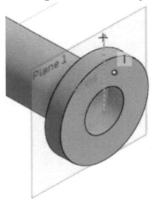

7. Right click and select **Escape line**.
8. On the toolbar, click **Constraints** drop-down > **Coincident**.
9. Select the sketch point and the endpoint construction line.

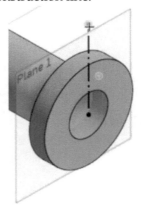

10. Apply dimension to the construction line, as shown.

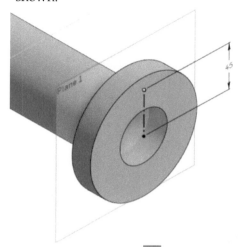

11. Click the green check ✅ on the **Sketch 4** dialog.
12. Activate the **Hole** command and select the sketch point.
13. Create a hole of 12 mm diameter on the *Extruded* feature.

14. On the Toolbar, click the **Linear pattern** drop-down > **Circular pattern** 🔘 .

15. On the **Circular pattern** dialog, click the **Pattern type > Feature pattern**.
16. Click on the **Features to pattern** selection box and select the 12 mm hole.
17. Click on the **Axis of pattern** selection box and select the outer circular face of the *Extruded* feature.
18. Type-in **360** and **6** in the **Angle** and **Instance count** fields, respectively.
19. Check the **Equal spacing** option and click the green check ✅ to pattern the hole.

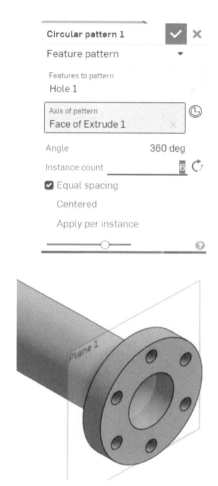

20. Create the *Extruded, Hole,* and *Circular pattern* features on the other end of the model.

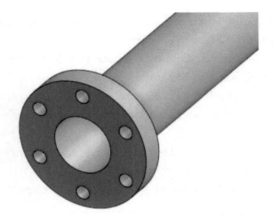

21. Click the **Document menu** located at the top-left corner of the window and click the **Close document** option to close the document.

Exercises
Exercise1

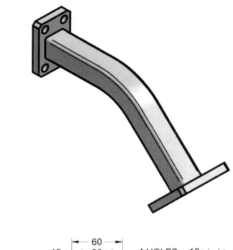

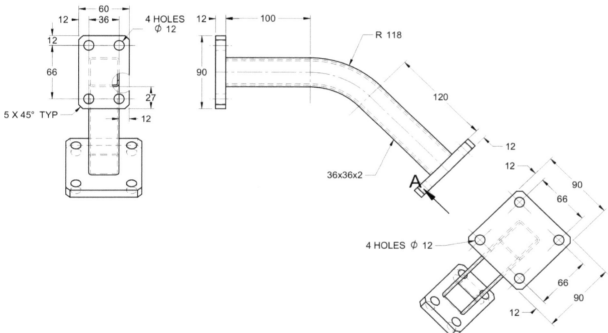

Chapter 7: Loft Features

Tutorial 1

In this example, you create the part shown below.

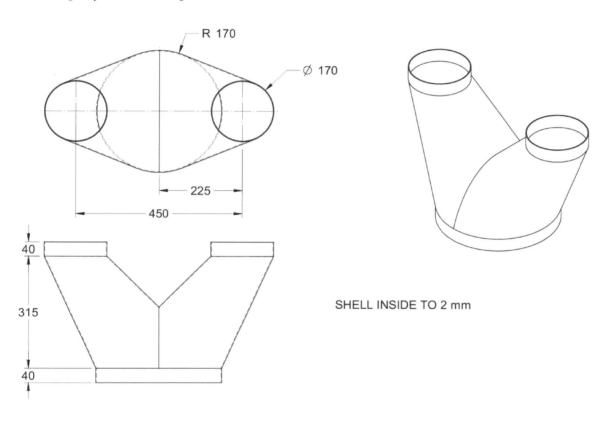

SHELL INSIDE TO 2 mm

Creating a New document

1. In your Internet Browser, go to https://www.onshape.com to start Onshape.

2. Next, click **SIGN IN** button located on the top right corner side of the web page. Enter the username and password, and then, click **Sign in**.

3. On the Documents page, click **Create > Folder**. Next, type Chapter 7 in the **Folder name** box and then click **Create**.

4. Double-click on the **Chapter 7** folder in the **Folders** section.

5. On the Documents page, click **Create > Document**; the **New document** dialog appears on the screen.

6. Enter Tutorial 1 in the **Document name** box and click **OK**; a new document appears.

7. Click the **Document menu** located at the top left corner of the window and select **Workspace Units**; the **Workspace Units** dialog appears on the screen.

8. On the **Workspace Units** dialog, select **Default length unit > Millimeter** and **Default mass unit > Gram**.

9. Leave the other default settings and click the green check ✓.

Creating a Loft Feature

1. Start a new sketch on the Top plane and draw a circle of **340** mm diameters.

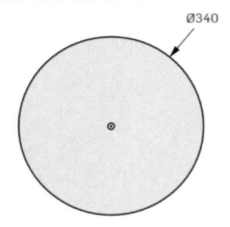

Ø340

2. Click the green check ✓ on the **Sketch 1** dialog.
3. Create an *Extruded* feature of **40** mm depth.

4. On the Toolbar, click the **Plane** ⬚ command.
5. Click on the top face of the geometry and type in **315** mm in the **Offset distance** field on the **Plane** dialog.
6. Click the green check ✓ to create an offset plane.
7. Start a sketch on the offset plane.
8. Draw a circle of **170** mm diameter and add dimensions to it, as shown.
9. Confirm the sketch.

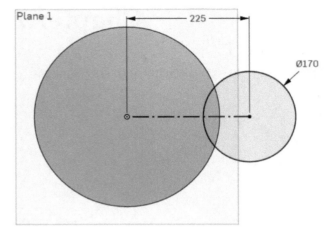

Plane 1 — 225 — Ø170

10. Deselect the sketch, if selected.
11. On the Toolbar, click the **Loft** 🔺 icon.
12. Select the circle.
13. Click on the circular edge of the base to define the second profile, as shown.

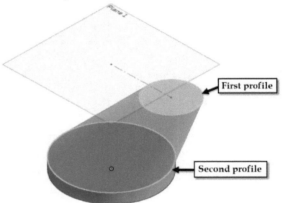

First profile

Second profile

14. Click the green check ✓ to create the *Loft* feature.

Extruding a Planar Face of the Model

1. Activate the **Extrude** command and click on the top face of the *Loft* feature.
2. On the **Extrude** dialog, type-in **40** mm in the **Depth** field.
3. Click the green check ✅ to create the *Extruded* feature.

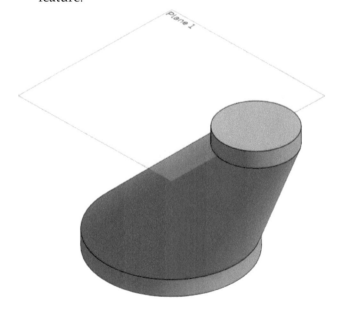

Mirroring the Entire Part

1. On the Toolbar, click the **Mirror** command and click the **Mirror type** drop-down **> Part mirror** on the **Mirror** dialog.
2. Select the model from the graphics area.
3. Click on the **Mirror plane** selection box and select the **Right** plane from the **Feature** window to define the mirroring plane.
4. Click the green check ✅ to mirror the entire solid body.

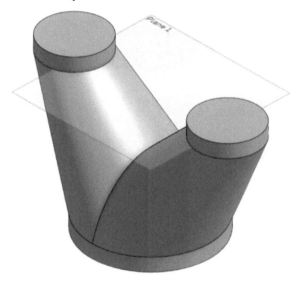

Shelling the Model geometry

1. On the Toolbar, click the **Shell** icon.
2. Click on the flat faces of the model geometry.

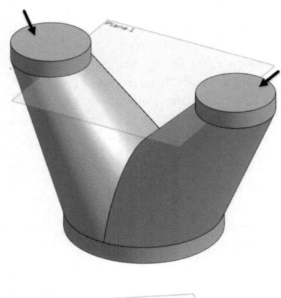

3. On the **Shell** dialog, type-in **2** in the **Shell Thickness** field.

4. Click the green check ✅ on the **Shell** dialog to shell the part geometry.

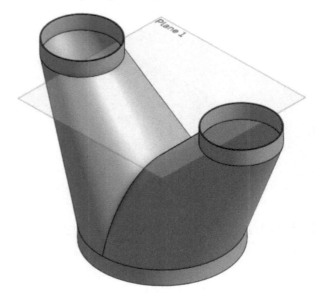

5. Click **Document menu > Close document** to close the document.

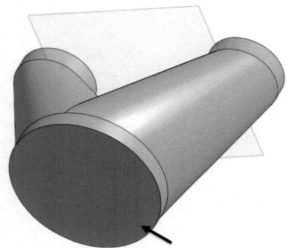

Exercises
Exercise 1

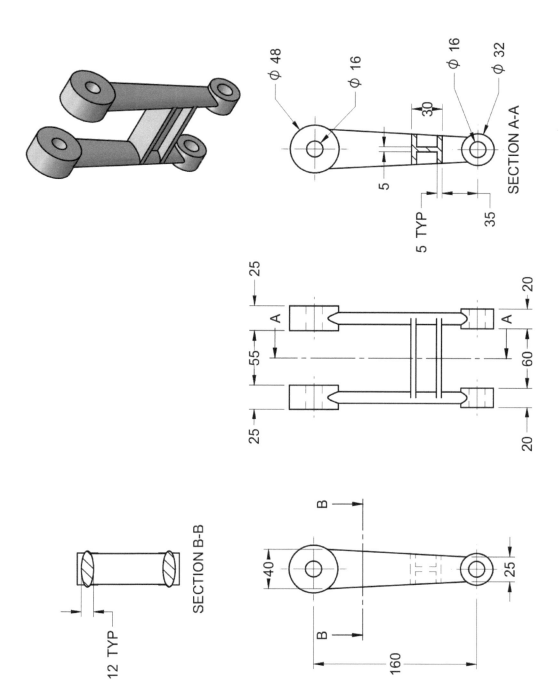

ø 48

ø 16

ø 16

ø 32

30

5

5 TYP

35

SECTION A-A

25

A

55

25

20

A

60

20

B

40

B

25

160

SECTION B-B

12 TYP

Chapter 8: Additional Features

Tutorial 1 (Millimetres)

In this example, you create the part shown next.

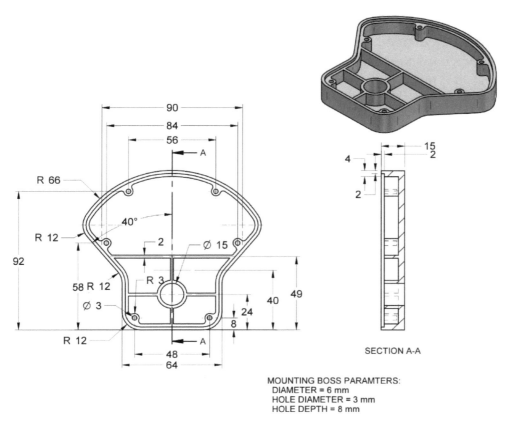

MOUNTING BOSS PARAMTERS:
 DIAMETER = 6 mm
 HOLE DIAMETER = 3 mm
 HOLE DEPTH = 8 mm

FILLET MOUNTING BOSS CORNER 2 mm

SECTION A-A

Creating a New document

1. In your Internet Browser, go to https://www.onshape.com to start Onshape.

2. Next, click **SIGN IN** button located on the top right corner side of the web page. Enter the username and password, and then, click **Sign in**.
3. On the Documents page, click **Create > Folder**. Next, type Chapter 8 in the **Folder name** box and then click **Create**.
4. Double-click on the **Chapter 8** folder in the Folders section.

5. On the Documents page, click **Create > Document**; the **New document** dialog appears on the screen.
6. Enter Tutorial 1 in the **Document name** box and click **OK**; a new document appears.
7. Click the **Document menu** located at the top left corner of the window and select **Workspace Units**; the **Workspace Units** dialog appears on the screen.
8. On the **Workspace Units** dialog, select **Default length unit > Millimeter** and **Default mass unit > Gram**.
9. Leave the other default settings and click the green check ✅.

Creating the Extruded Feature

1. Click the **Sketch** command on the Toolbar and start a new sketch on the **Top** plane.
2. On the Toolbar, click the **Line** command and draw the sketch, as shown in the figure below.
3. Click the **Mirror** ⊟ command on the Toolbar, and then mirror the vertical and inclined line about the construction line. Next, apply the **Coincident** ⋌ constraints between the endpoints, as shown.

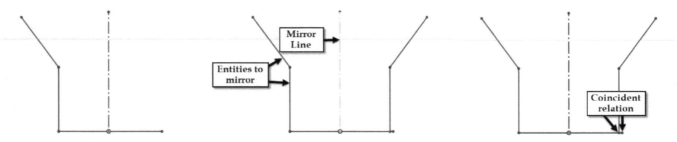

4. On the Toolbar, click the **3-point arc** command, and then create an arc by specifying the points in the sequence, as shown.
5. Apply dimensions to the sketch, as shown.

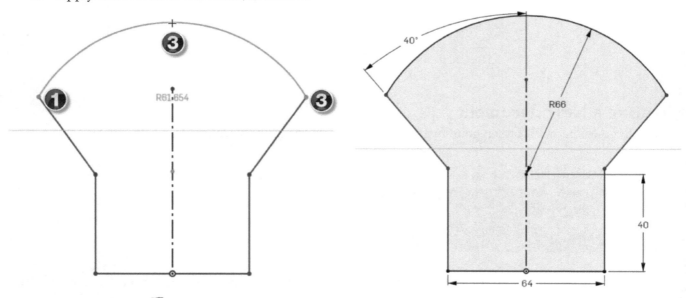

6. Click the **Fillet** ⌒ command on the Toolbar, and then select the sharp corners to fillet.
7. Press **Enter** and type **12** in the **Radius** box. Again, press **Enter** to update the radius.
8. On the Toolbar, click the **Dimension** command. Add a linear dimension between the centerpoints of the fillets, as shown.

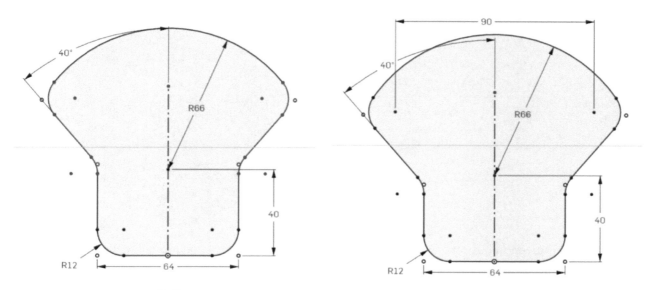

9. Click the green check ✅ on the **Sketch1** dialog to confirm the sketch.

10. Activate the **Extrude** 📦 command and create the *Extrude* feature of 14 mm depth.
11. Create the *Shell* feature of 4 mm depth.

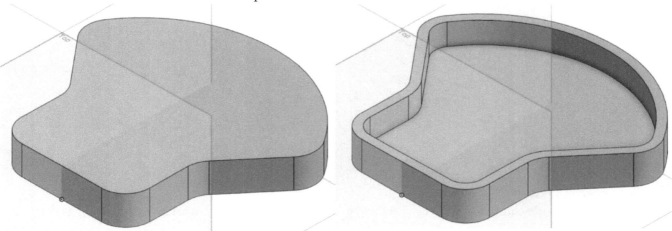

Adding a Lip to the model

1. On the toolbar, click the **Sketch** command and select the top face of the shell feature, as shown.

2. On the toolbar, click the **Offset** command.

3. Right click on the graphics area and select **Create selection**.

4. On the **Create selection** dialog, click the **Edges** tab and select the **Tangent connected** option from the drop-own. Next, select any one of the outer edges of the model.

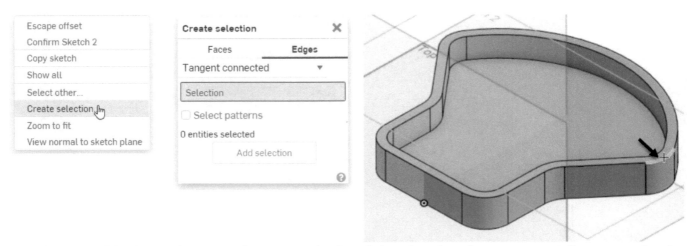

5. Click the **Add selection** button on the **Create selection** dialog; the edges that are tangentially connected to the selected edge are added to the selection.
6. Click on the graphics area and type 2 in the offset distance value box and press Enter.

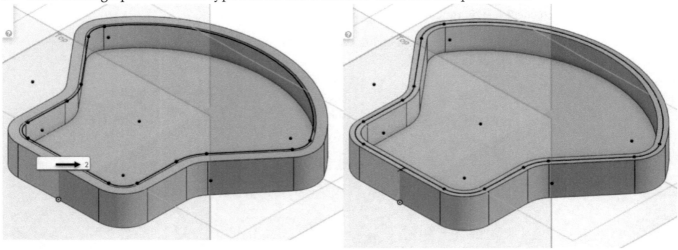

7. Click the green check on the **Sketch 2** dialog.
8. Activate the **Extrude** command and click on the region enclosed by the sketch and inner edge of the shell feature.
9. Click the **Remove** tab on the **Extrude 2** dialog.
10. Select **End type > Blind** and enter **2** in the **Depth** box and click **OK** to create the extruded cut feature.

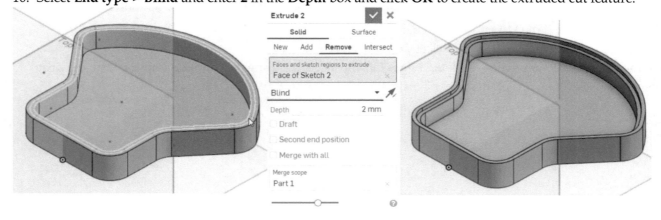

Creating Bosses

1. On the toolbar, click the **Sketch** command, and then click on the bottom face of the extruded cut feature.
2. Draw the three circles on the sketch plane. Next, click **Constraints** drop-down > **Equal** = on the toolbar.
3. Select the first two circles to make them equal in diameter. Next, select the second and third circles to make them equal.
4. Add dimensions to them, as shown. Click the green check on the **Sketch 3** dialog.

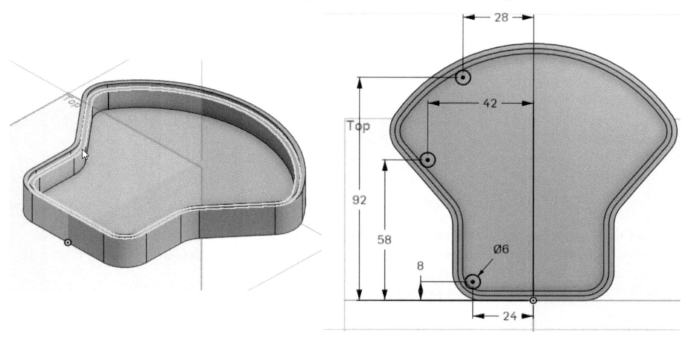

5. On the toolbar, click the **Extrude** command. Click inside the circles.
6. Click the **Add** tab on the **Extrude 3** dialog.
7. On the **Extrude 3** dialog, click **End type > Up to face** and select the bottom surface of the *Shell* feature, as shown.

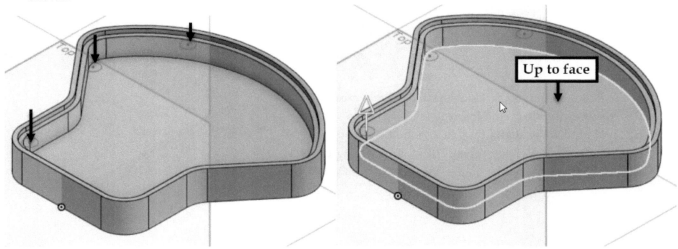

8. Check the **Draft** option and type-in **1** in the **Draft angle** box.

9. Click the green check on the dialog to create the *Extrude* feature.

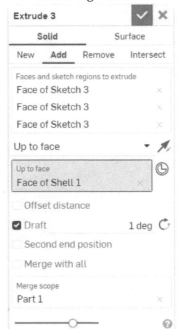
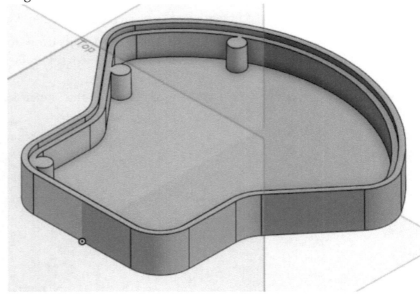

10. Click the **Sketch** command on the toolbar and select the bottom face of the extruded cut feature, as shown.
11. Create circles and apply the **Equal** constraint between them. Also, apply the **Concentric** constraint between the circles and circular edges of the extruded features.
12. Click the green check on the **Sketch 4** dialog.

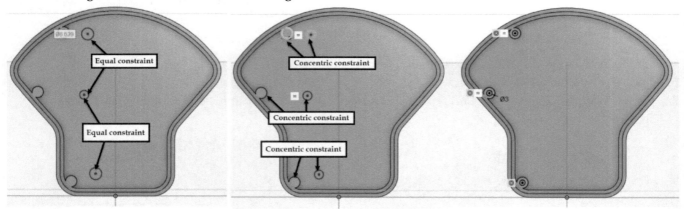

13. Click **Extrude** on the toolbar and select the newly created circles.
14. Click the **Remove** tab on the **Extrude 4** dialog.
15. Click **End type > Blind** and type-in 8 in the **Depth** box.
16. Check the **Draft** option and type-in **1** in the **Draft angle** box.
17. Click the green check on the dialog to create the *Extrude* feature.

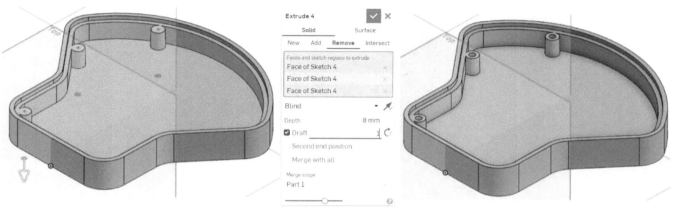

18. On the toolbar, click the **Mirror** command. Next, select **Mirror type > Feature Mirror** on the **Mirror** dialog.
19. Click the **Features to mirror** selection button and select the *Extrude* and *Cut* features from the Features window.
20. Click the **Mirror plane** selection button and select the **Right** plane on the coordinate system.
21. Click the green check to mirror the extrude features.

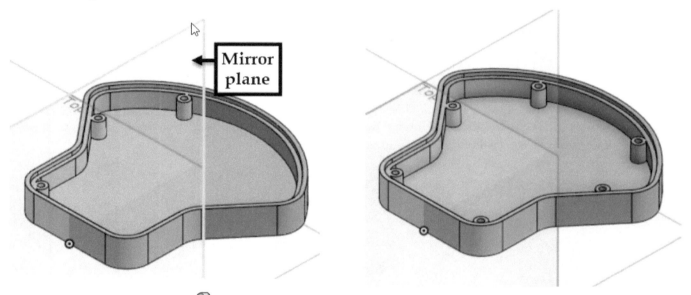

22. On the toolbar, click **Fillet** 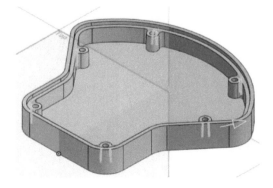 command and select the edges where the extruded features meet the walls of the geometry.

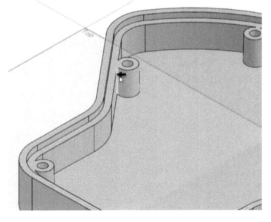

23. Type **2** in the **Radius** box. Click the green check to fillet the selected edges.

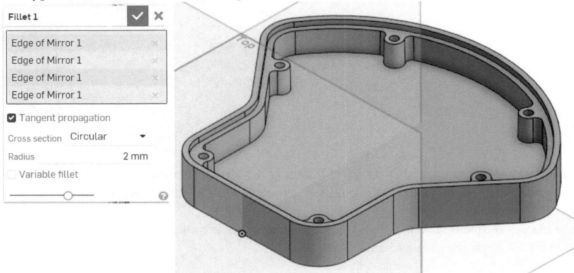

Creating the Rib feature

1. On the toolbar, click the **Sketch** command and select the bottom face of the extruded cut feature.
2. Click the **Center Point Circle** command on the toolbar and create a circle, as shown.
3. Click the Line command on the toolbar and select the midpoint of the lower horizontal edge, as shown. Next, move the pointer vertically upward and click to create a vertical line.
4. On the toolbar, click **Constraints** drop-down > **Midpoint**. Next, select the center point of the circle and the vertical line; the circle is constrained to the midpoint of the line.

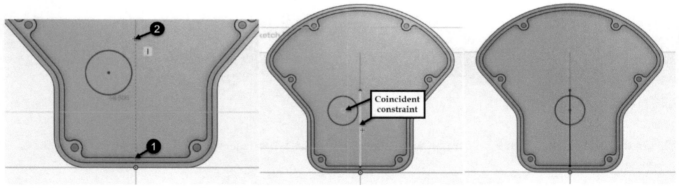

5. Click the **Line** command on the toolbar and create two horizontal lines, as shown.
6. On the toolbar, click **Constraints** drop-down > **Midpoint**. Next, select any one of the horizontal line and the centerpoint of the circle; the centerpoint of the circle is constrained to the midpoint of the horizontal line.
7. Select the other horizontal line and the endpoint of the vertical line; the endpoint of the vertical line is constrained to the midpoint of the horizontal line.
8. Add dimensions to the sketch, as shown.

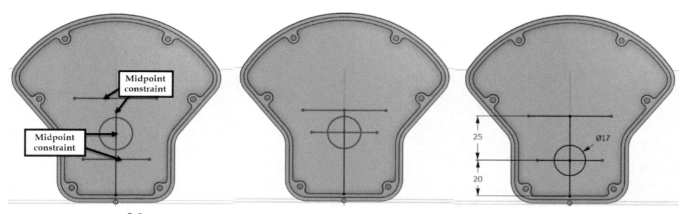

9. Click the **Trim** ✂ command on the toolbar and select the lines inside the circle, as shown.

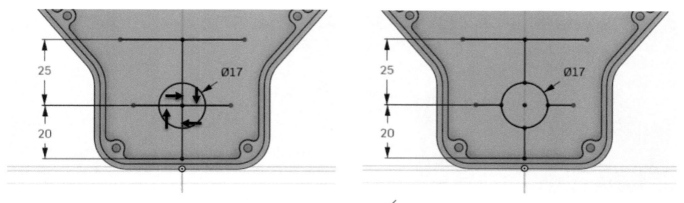

10. On the toolbar, click **Constraints** drop-down > **Coincident** ⟨⟩. Next, select the endpoint of the horizontal line.

11. Select the model edge to constrain the endpoint coincident with it, as shown.

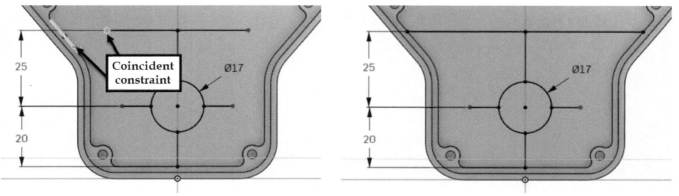

12. Likewise, apply the **Coincident** constraint between the other endpoint of the horizontal line and the model edge, as shown.

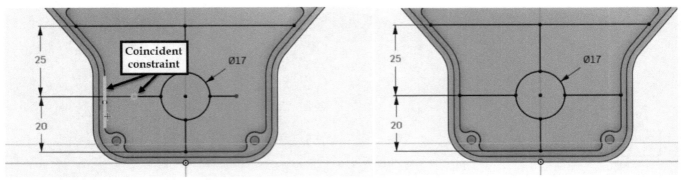

13. Click the green check on the **Sketch 5** dialog.
14. On the toolbar, click the **Rib** command and select the entities of the sketch.
15. On the **Rib** dialog, select **Rib extrusion direction > Normal to sketch plane**.
16. Type **1** in the **Thickness** box to specify the rib thickness.
17. Check the **Merge ribs** option and click **OK** to create the *Rib* feature.

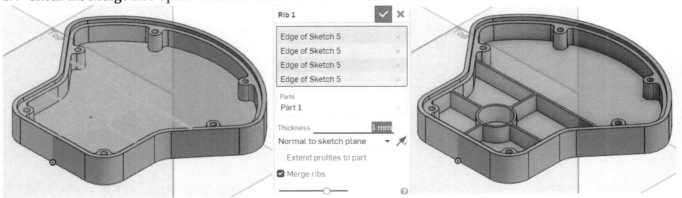

18. Close the file.

Tutorial 2 (Inches)

In this example, you create the part shown next.

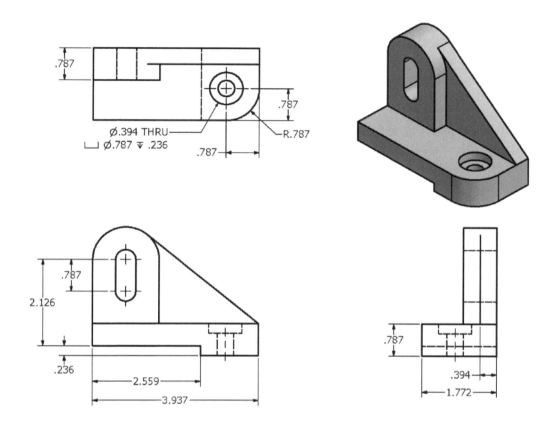

Creating a New document

1. In your Internet Browser, go to https://www.onshape.com to start Onshape.

2. Next, click **SIGN IN** button located on the top right corner side of the web page. Enter the username and password, and then, click **Sign in**.
3. Double-click on the **Chapter 8** folder in the **Folders** section.
4. On the Documents page, click **Create > Document**; the **New document** dialog appears on the screen.
5. Enter Tutorial 2 in the **Document name** box and click **OK**; a new document appears.
6. Click the **Document menu** located at the top left corner of the window and select **Workspace Units**; the **Workspace Units** dialog appears on the screen.
7. On the **Workspace Units** dialog, select **Default length unit > Inch** and **Default mass unit > Pound**.
8. Leave the other default settings and click the green check ✅.

Creating the Extruded features

1. Click the **Sketch** command on the Toolbar and start a new sketch on the **Top** plane.
2. Click the **Corner rectangle** command on the toolbar and select the origin point of the sketch. Next, move the pointer toward the right and click.
3. Click the Dimension command on the toolbar and apply dimensions to the rectangle, as shown.
4. Click the green check on the Sketch 1 dialog.
5. On the toolbar, click the **Extrude** 🗐 command and select the rectangular sketch.
6. On the **Extrude 1** dialog, select **End type > Blind** and enter 0.787 in the **Depth** box. Click the green check to create the *Extrude* feature.

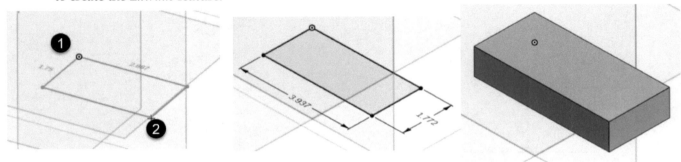

7. Activate the **Sketch** command and select the **Front** plane.
8. Right-click and select **View normal to sketch plane**; the sketch plane orients normal to the screen.
9. Click the **Corner Rectangle** ⬜ command on the toolbar and specify the first and second corners of the rectangle, as shown.

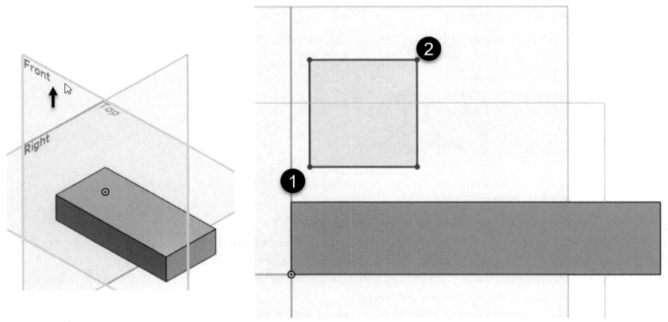

10. On the toolbar, click **Arc** drop-down **> Tangent arc**. Next, select the left vertical line of the rectangle.
11. Move the pointer toward the right and select the top right corner point of the rectangle.

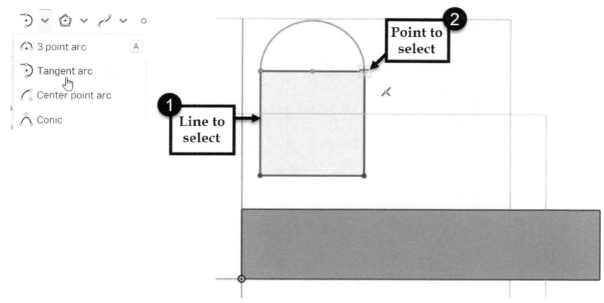

12. Click the **Trim** ✄ command on the toolbar and select the horizontal line of the rectangle, as shown.

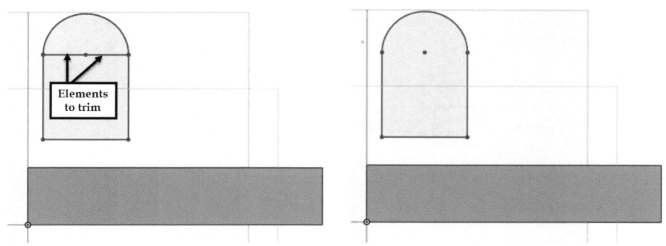

13. Apply the **Coincident** constraint between the horizontal line of the sketch and the top horizontal edge, as shown.

14. Likewise, apply the **Coincident** constraint between the left vertical line of the sketch and the left vertical edge of the model.

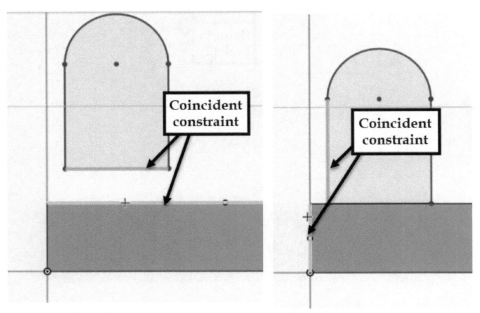

15. On the toolbar, click **Constraints** drop-down > **Tangent** and select the arc and the right vertical line of the sketch.

16. Click the **Dimension** command on the toolbar and create dimensions, as shown. Next, click the green check on the **Sketch 2** dialog.

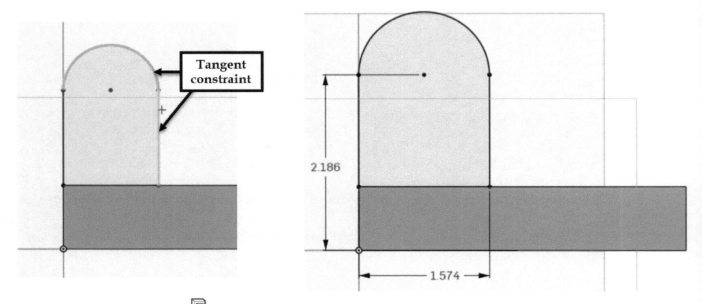

17. Activate the **Extrude** command and select the sketch. On the **Extrude 2** dialog, select **End type > Blind** and enter 0.787 in the **Depth** box. Click the green check to complete the Extrude feature.

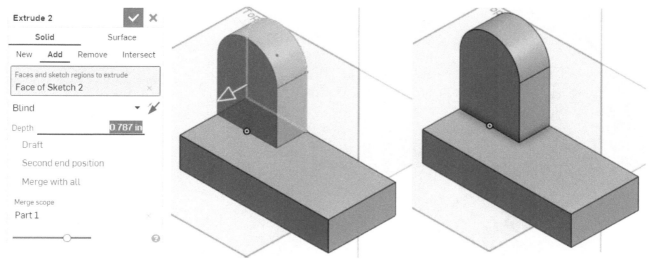

Creating the Rib feature

1. On the toolbar, click the **Plane** command and select the Front plane from the graphics area.
2. Select **Plane type > Offset** from the **Plane 1** dialog. Next, type **0.197** in the **Offset distance** box, and then click the green check.

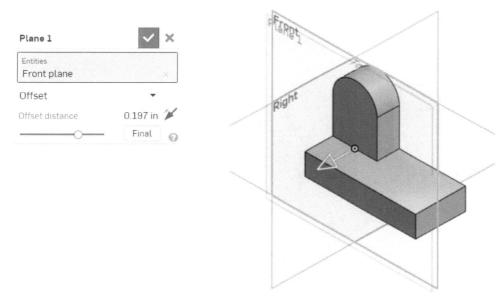

3. Activate the **Sketch** command and select the newly created plane. Draw an inclined line, as shown.

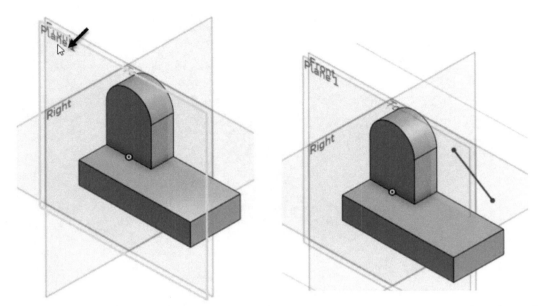

4. On the toolbar, click **Constraints** drop-down **> Tangent**, and then select the inclined line and the curved edge; the line is made tangent to the edge.
5. On the toolbar, click **Constraints** drop-down **> Coincident**, and then select the endpoint of the inclined line and the curved edge; the endpoint of the line is made coincident to the edge.
6. Likewise, make the other endpoint of the line coincident with the vertex point, as shown. Click the green check on the **Sketch 3** dialog.

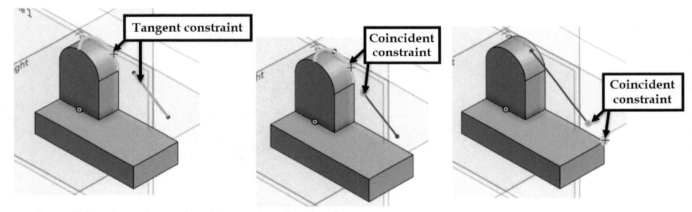

7. Click **Rib** on the toolbar. Next, select the sketch.
8. On the **Rib** dialog, select **Rib extrusion direction > Parallel to sketch plane**.
9. Type-in 0.394 in the **Thickness** box. Next, click the green check to create the *Rib* feature.

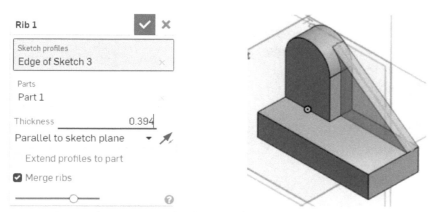

Rib 1 ✓ ✕

Sketch profiles
Edge of Sketch 3 ✕

Parts
Part 1

Thickness   0.394
Parallel to sketch plane ▾ ✦
  Extend profiles to part
☑ Merge ribs

Creating the Extruded Cut features

1. Activate the **Sketch** command and click on the front face of the second feature, as shown.
2. On the toolbar, click the **Line** command.
3. Place the pointer near the centerpoint of the curved edge; the centerpoint is highlighted in orange.
4. Click to select the centerpoint of the curved edge. Next, move the pointer downward and click to specify the second center of the line.
5. Right click and select **Escape line**.

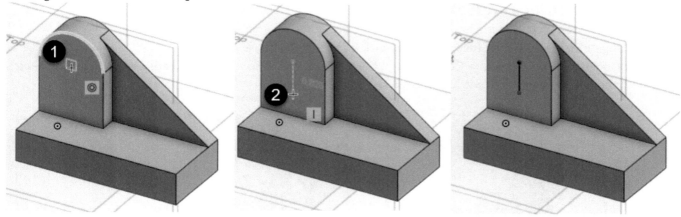

6. On the toolbar, click **Offset** drop-down > **Slot**. Next, select the line created in the previous step.
7. Click on the dimension and enter .474 in the value box.
8. Add dimension to the vertical line, and then convert it into a construction element.

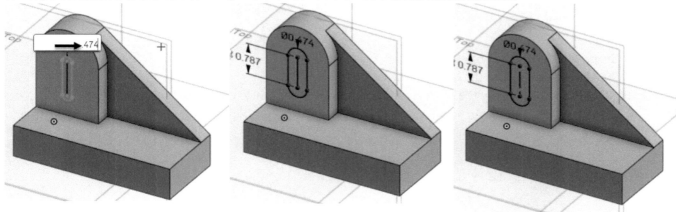

9. Click the green check on the **Sketch 4** dialog.

10. Activate the **Extrude** 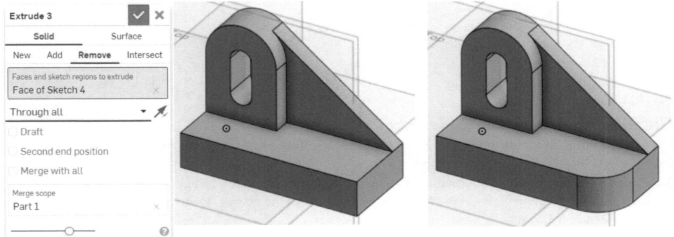 command and select the sketch.
11. On the **Extrude 3** dialog, click the **Remove** tab and select **End type > Through all**.
12. Click the green check to create the *Extruded cut* feature.
13. Add a fillet of 0.787 in radius to the right vertical edge of the rectangular base.

Creating the Fillet and Hole features

1. Activate the **Sketch** command and click on the top face of the first feature.
2. Click the **Point** command on the toolbar and click on the sketch plane.
3. Click **Constraints** drop-down > **Concentric** on the toolbar. Next, select the curved edge of the fillet and sketch point; the point is made concentric to the fillet.

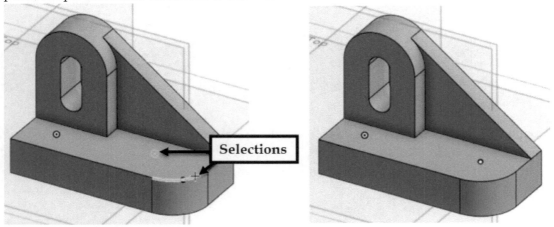

4. Click the green check on the **Sketch 5** dialog.
5. Click the **Hole** command on the toolbar and select the sketch point.
6. On the **Hole 1** dialog, specify the settings, as shown. Next, click **OK** to create the hole.

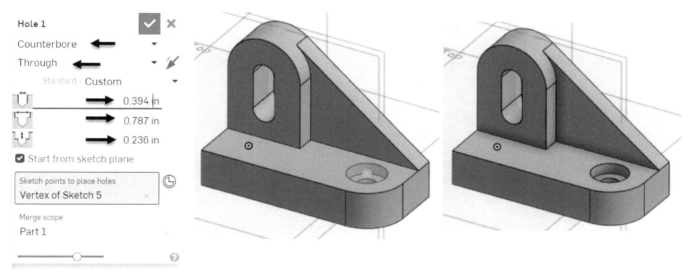

7. Activate the **Sketch** command and select the front face of the rectangular base.
8. Draw a sketch and add dimensions to it. Click the green check on the **Sketch 6** dialog.
9. Create an *Extruded Cut* feature using the sketch.

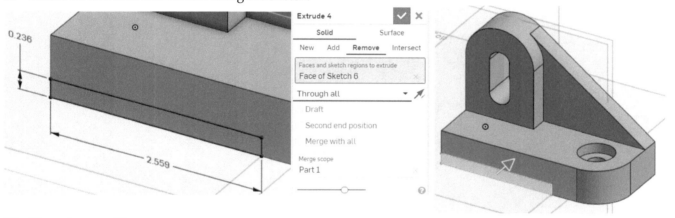

10. Close the part file.

Exercises

Exercise 1

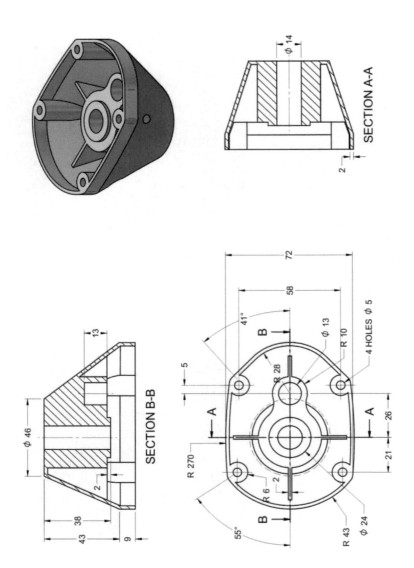

SECTION A-A

SECTION B-B

Exercise 2

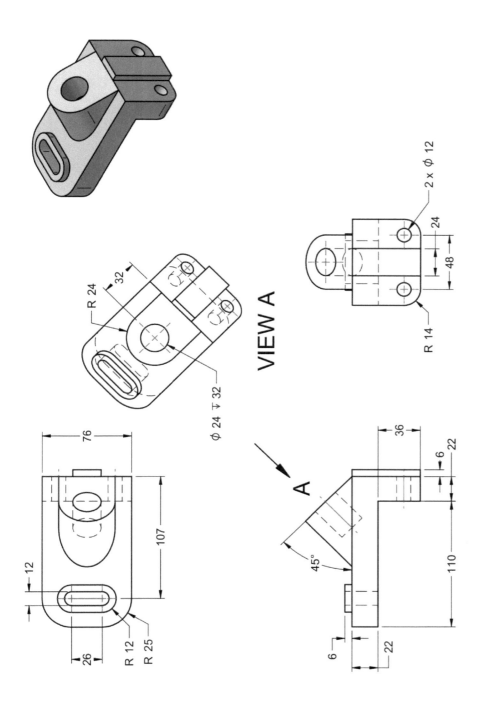

VIEW A

2 x ⌀ 12

24

48

R 14

R 24

32

⌀ 24 ▽ 32

A

36

6

22

45°

110

6

22

76

107

12

26

R 12

R 25

107

Exercise 3 (Inches)

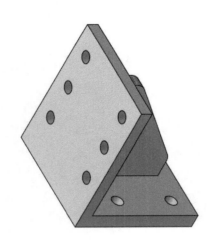

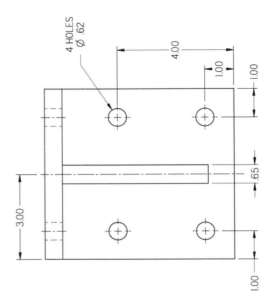

4 HOLES Ø .62 — 4.00 — 1.00 — 1.00 — 3.00 — .65 — 1.00

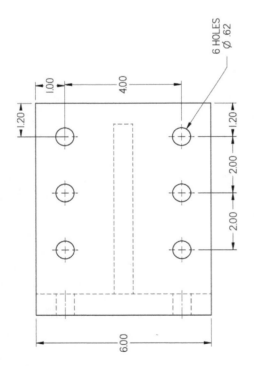

6 HOLES Ø .62 — 1.00 — 4.00 — 1.20 — 1.20 — 2.00 — 2.00 — 6.00

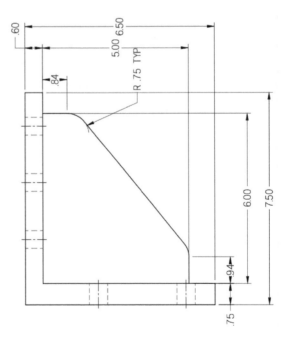

.60 — 6.50 — 5.00 — .84 — R .75 TYP — 6.00 — 7.50 — .94 — .75

108

Chapter 9: Modifying Parts

In the design process, it is not required to achieve the final model in the first attempt. There is always a need to modify the existing parts to get the desired part geometry. In this chapter, you learn various commands and techniques to make changes to a part.

Tutorial 1 (Inches)

In this example, you create the part shown below and then modify it.

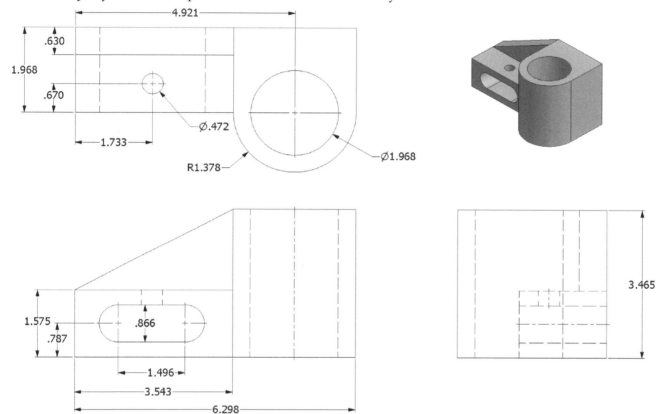

Creating a New document

1. In your Internet Browser, go to https://www.onshape.com to start Onshape.

2. Next, click **SIGN IN** button located on the top right corner side of the web page. Enter the username and password, and then, click **Sign in**.

3. On the Documents page, click **Create > Folder**. Next, type Chapter 9 in the **Folder name** box and then click **Create**.
4. Double-click on the **Chapter 9** folder in the **Folders** section.
5. On the Documents page, click **Create > Document**; the **New document** dialog appears on the screen.
6. Enter Tutorial 1 in the **Document name** box and click **OK**; a new document appears.
7. Click the **Document menu** located at the top left corner of the window and select **Workspace Units**; the **Workspace Units** dialog appears on the screen.
8. On the **Workspace Units** dialog, select **Default length unit > Inch** and **Default mass unit > Pound**.
9. Leave the other default settings and click the green check ✓.
10. Create the part using the tools and commands available in Onshape, as shown in the figure. You can also download this file from the companion website.

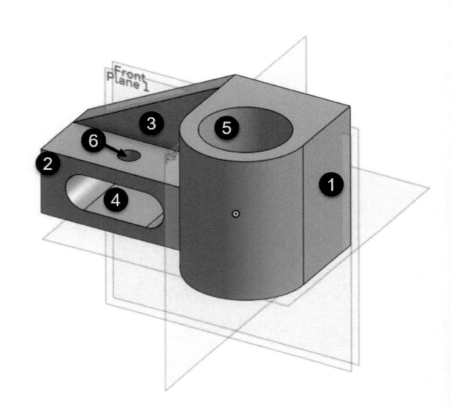

Editing a Feature

1. Click right mouse button on the **Hole 1** in the **Features** window and click **Edit**. On the **Hole 1** dialog, select **Style > Counterbore**.
2. Select **Standard > Custom** and enter **1.378, 1.968,** and **0.787** in the **Diameter, Counterbore diameter**, and **Counterbore depth** fields, respectively. Click the green check ✓.

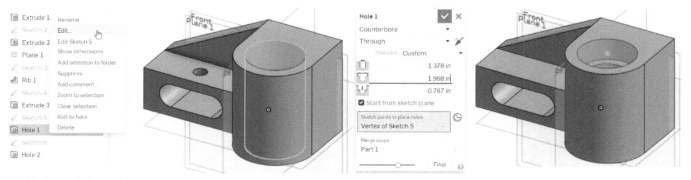

Editing Sketches

1. Right-click on the *Sketch 2* in the **Features** window and select **Edit**. Modify the sketch, as shown. Click **green check** ✅.

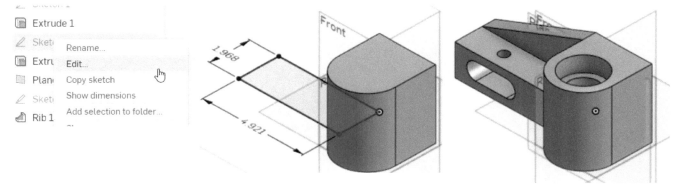

2. Right click on the slot and select **Edit Sketch 4**.
3. Delete the length dimension of the slot, and then add a new dimension between the right-side arc and right vertical edge.

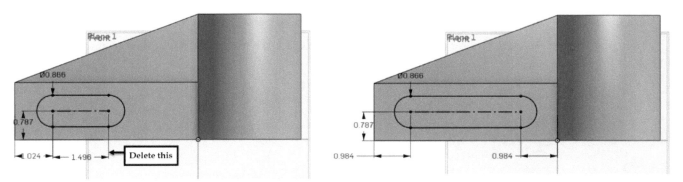

4. Delete the dimension between the centerline of the slot and the horizontal edge.
5. Apply the **Coincident** constraint between the construction line of the slot and the midpoint of the left vertical edge. Click the green check ✅ on the **Sketch 4** dialog.

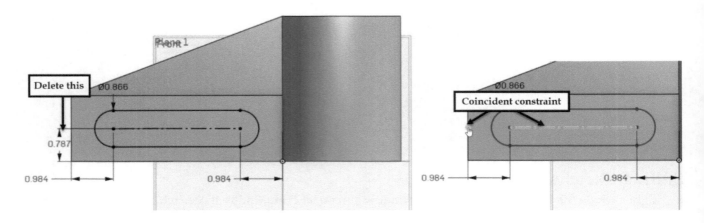

6. Right-click on the small hole, and then select the **Edit Sketch 6** from the menu. Delete the positioning dimensions.

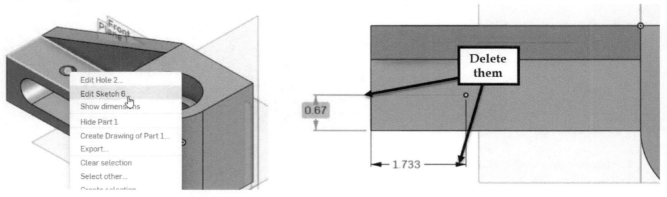

7. Create a construction line and make its ends coincident with the corners, as shown below.

8. On the Toolbar, click the **Midpoint** ⌀ icon, and select the hole point. Next, select the construction line; the hole point becomes the midpoint of the construction line. Click the green check ✓ on the **Sketch 6** dialog.

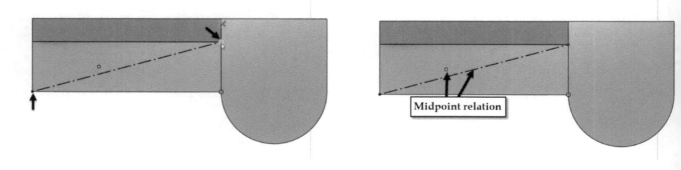

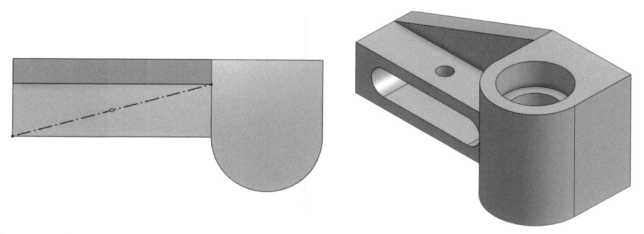

9. Now, change the size of the rectangular extruded feature. Notice that the slot and hole are adjusted automatically.

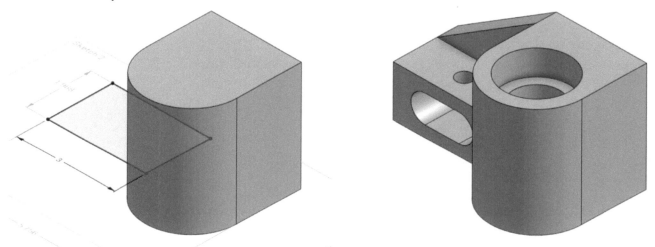

10. Click the **Document menu** located on the top left corner of the window and click the **Close document** to close the document.

Tutorial 2 (Millimetres)

In this example, you create the part shown below and then modify it using the editing tools.

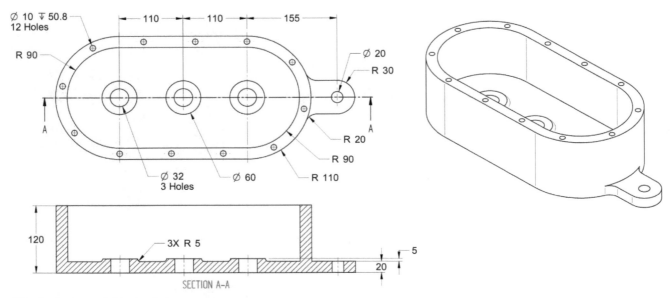

Creating a New document

1. In your Internet Browser, go to https://www.onshape.com to start Onshape.

2. Next, click **SIGN IN** button located on the top right corner side of the web page. Enter the username and password, and then, click **Sign in**.
3. Double-click on the **Chapter 8** folder in the **Folders** section.
4. On the Documents page, click **Create > Document**; the **New document** dialog appears on the screen.
5. Enter Tutorial 2 in the **Document name** box and click **OK**; a new document appears.
6. Click the **Document menu** located at the top left corner of the window and select **Workspace Units**; the **Workspace Units** dialog appears on the screen.
7. On the **Workspace Units** dialog, select **Default length unit > Millimeter** and **Default mass unit > Gram**.
8. Leave the other default settings and click the green check [✓].

Creating the Extruded and Shell Features

1. Activate the **Sketch** command and select the **Top** plane from the graphics area.
2. Click a horizontal line and apply the **Midpoint** constraint between the line and origin.
3. Click the **Offset** drop-down > **Slot** on the toolbar and select the line. Next, click in the graphics area to create a slot.
4. Select the line used to create the slot, and then click the **Construction** command on the toolbar.
5. Click the **Dimension** command on the toolbar and apply dimensions to the slot. Next, click the green check on the **Sketch 1** dialog.

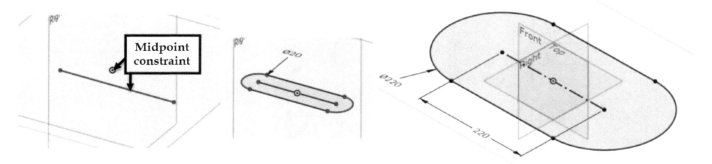

6. Click the **Extrude** command on the toolbar and select the slot. Next, type **120** in the **Depth** box and click the green check on the **Extrude 1** dialog.

7. Click the **Shell** ⬜ command on the toolbar and select the top face of the model. Type **20** in the **Shell thickness** box and click the green check.

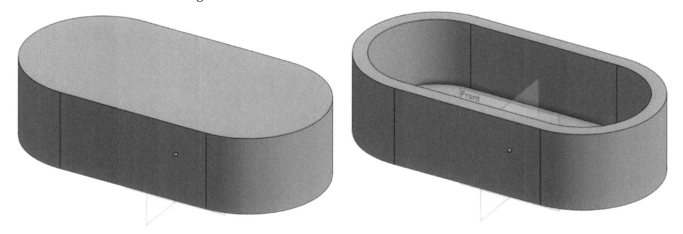

Adding the Extruded and Hole features

1. Click the **Sketch** command and select the Top plane from the **Features** window.

2. Click the **Use (Project/Convert)** ⬜ command on the toolbar. Next, select the circular edge of the model, as shown.

3. Create two lines and arc using the **Line** and **3 point arc** commands, respectively.

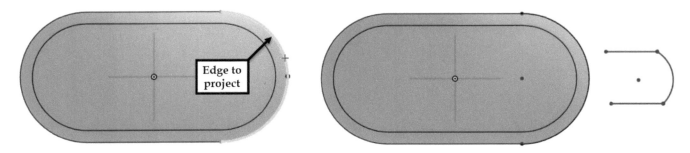

4. Apply the **Equal** constraint between the two lines.

5. Apply the **Tangent** constraint between the arc and the two lines.

6. Apply the **Coincident** constraint between the endpoints of the lines and the projected edge.

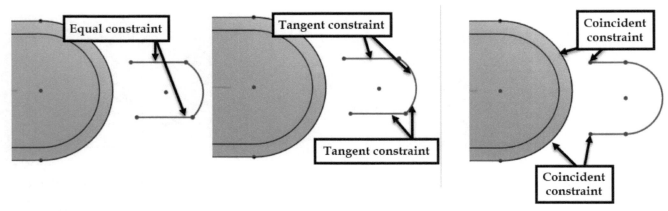

7. Add dimensions to the sketch, as shown.

8. Click the **Trim** ⌘ command on the toolbar and select the portions of the projected entity, as shown. Next, click the green check on the **Sketch 2** dialog.

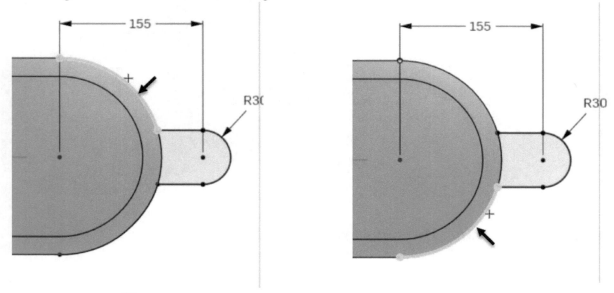

9. Click the **Extrude** command on the toolbar and select the newly created sketch.

10. Type **20** in the **Depth** box and click the green check on the **Extrude 2** dialog.

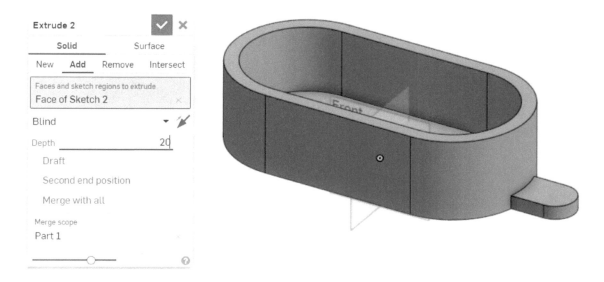

11. Create a hole of 20 mm diameter on the newly created extruded feature.

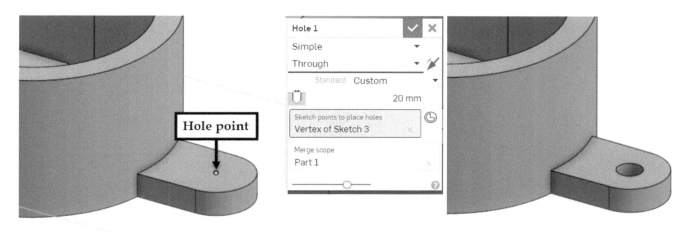

12. Create an extruded feature of 5 mm depth on the inner bottom face of the shell feature.

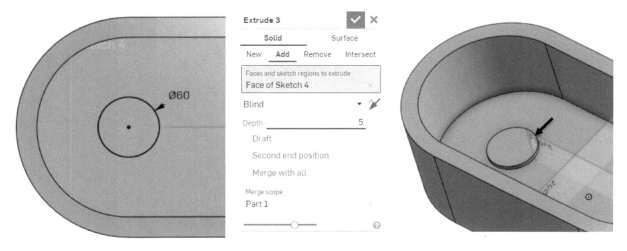

13. Create a hole of 32 mm diameter on the newly created extruded feature.

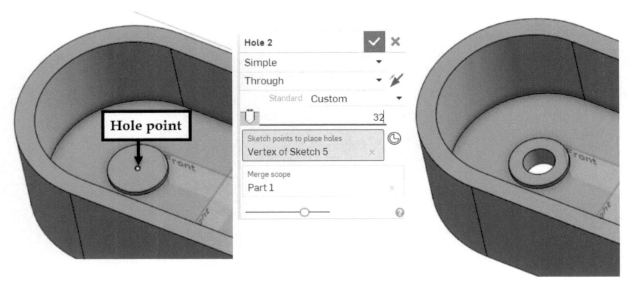

Creating the Linear Pattern

1. Click the **Linear Pattern** command on the toolbar and select the Feature pattern option from the Pattern type drop-down available on the Linear pattern 1 dialog.
2. Select the newly created extruded feature and the hole, as shown.
3. Click the **Direction** selection box and select the edge of the model, as shown.

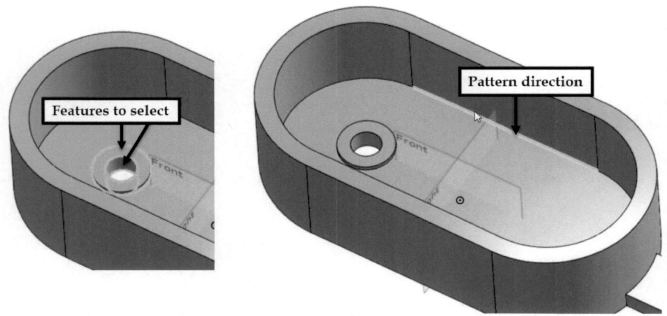

4. Type 110 and 3 in the **Distance** and **Instant count** boxes, respectively. Next, click the green check on the **Linear pattern 1** dialog.

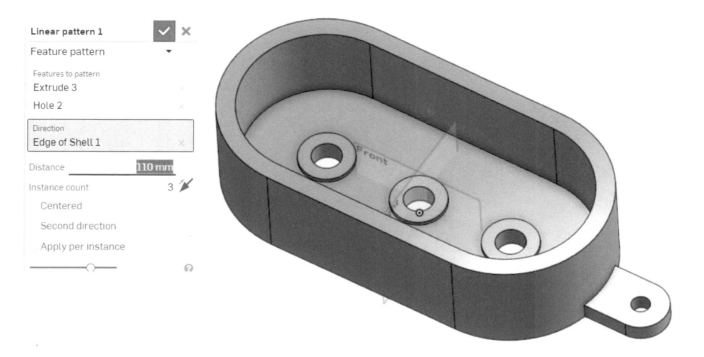

Linear pattern 1 ✓ ✗

Feature pattern ▾

Features to pattern
Extrude 3
Hole 2

Direction
Edge of Shell 1 ✗

Distance   **110 mm**

Instance count   3

Centered

Second direction

Apply per instance

Creating the Curve pattern

1. Click the **Sketch** command on the toolbar and select the top face of the model, as shown.
2. Place a point and add dimensions to it, as shown. Next, click the green check on the **Sketch 6** dialog.

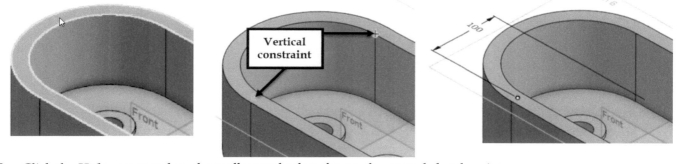

Vertical constraint

3. Click the **Hole** command on the toolbar and select the newly created sketch point.
4. Specify the parameters on the **Hole 1** dialog, as shown. Next, click the green check to complete the **Hole** feature.

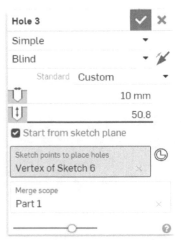

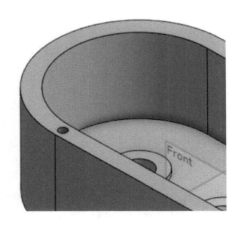

5. On the toolbar, click the **Pattern** drop-down > **Curve pattern**. Next, select the **Feature pattern** option from the **Pattern type** drop-down.

6. Select the newly created hole from the model. Next, click the **Path to pattern along** selection box from the **Curve pattern 1** dialog.

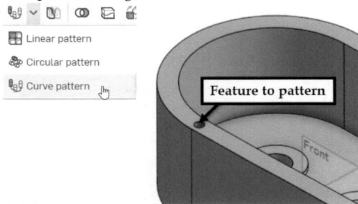

7. Right click and select **Create selection** from the shortcut menu. Next, select **Tangent connected** from the drop-down available on the **Create selection** dialog.

8. Click the inner circular edge of the shell feature, as shown; the edges that are connected tangently to the selected edge are highlighted.

9. Click the **Add selection** button on the **Create selection** dialog. Next, close the **Create selection** dialog.

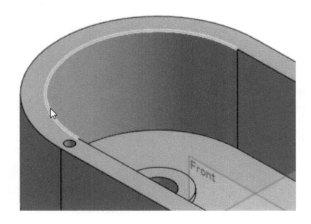

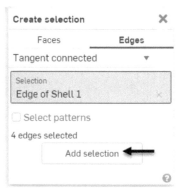

10. Type 12 in the **Instant count** box and click the green check on the **Curve pattern 1** dialog.

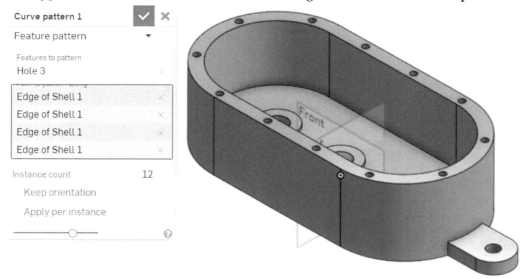

Creating the Fillet features

1. Click the **Fillet** command on the toolbar and select the edges of the model, as shown.
2. Type 20 in the **Radius** box and click the green check.

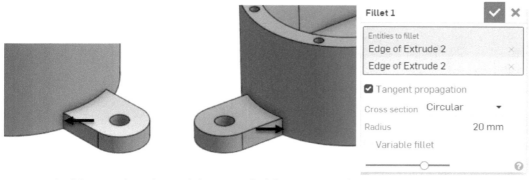

3. Apply fillets to the edges of the extruded features, as shown.

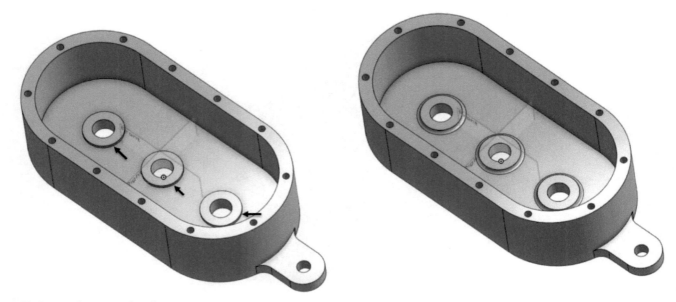

Editing the Hole feature

1. Click on the 20 mm diameter hole, and then click **Edit Hole 2**; the **dialog** appears.
2. On the **Hole** dialog, select **Style > Counterbore**.
3. On the **Hole** dialog, enter 20, 30, and 10 in the Diameter, Counterbore diameter, and Counterbore depth boxes, respectively. Click the green check to close the dialog.

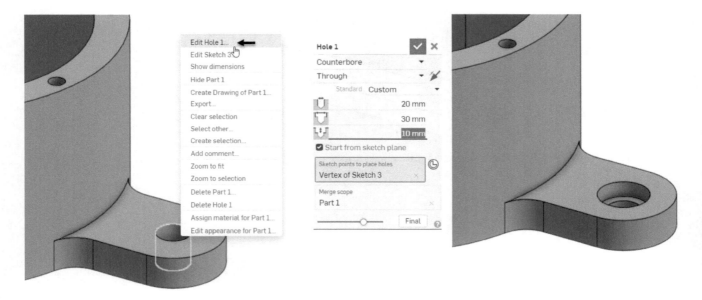

Moving Faces

1. On the Toolbar, click the **Move Face** command, and then select **Translate** from the **Move face type** drop-down available on the **Move face 1** dialog.
2. Click on the round faces of the counterbore hole. Next, the cylindrical face concentric to it.
3. Click the **Direction** selection button on the dialog. Next, select the edge of the extruded feature, as shown.

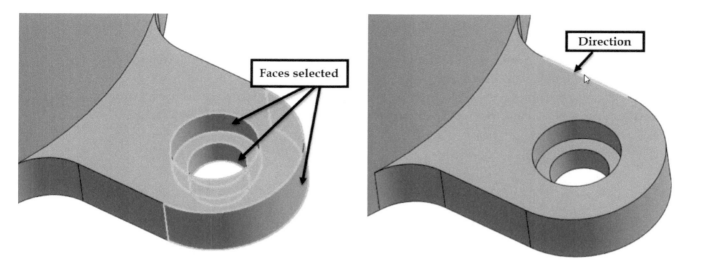

4. Type **20** in the **Distance** box and click the green check on the **Move face 1** dialog.

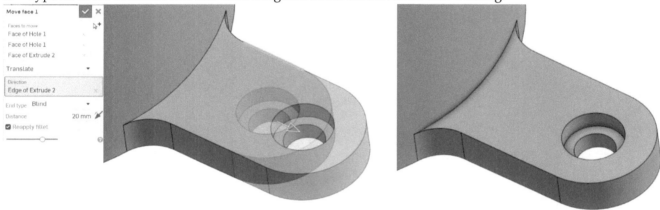

Editing the Curve pattern

1. Right click on any one of the holes of the curve pattern, and then select **Edit Curve pattern 1**.
2. Type 14 in the **Instance count** box and click the green check to update the pattern.

3. On the Toolbar, click **the Move Face** command, and then select **Translate** from the **Move face type** drop-down available on the **Move face 2** dialog.
4. Right-click and select **Create selection** from the shortcut menu — next, select **Hole** from the drop-down available on the **Create selection** dialog.
5. Select any one of the holes of the curve pattern, and then check the **Select patterns** option from the **Create selection** dialog. Next, click the **Add selection** button and close the **Create selection** dialog.

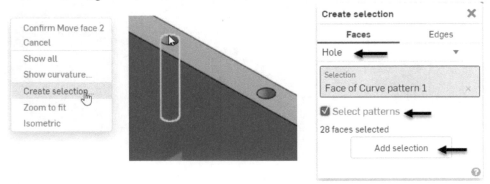

6. Select the top face of the model to add it to the selection.

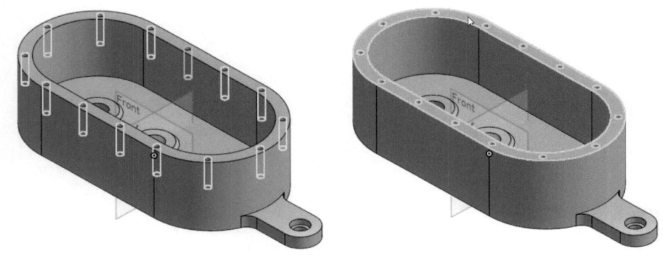

7. Click the **Direction** selection button and select the vertical edge of the model, as shown.

8. Type 40 in the **Distance** box and click the **Reverse direction** icon next to it.

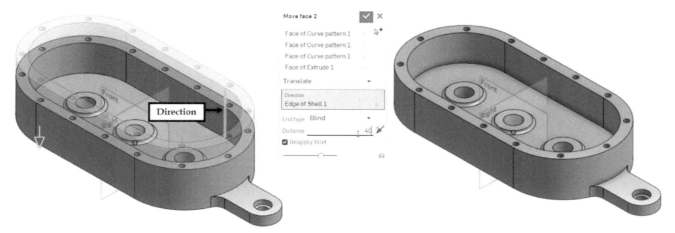

9. Close the document.

Exercises

Exercise 1

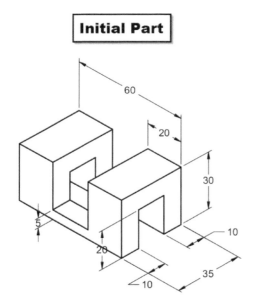

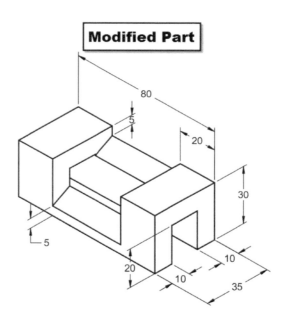

Exercise 2

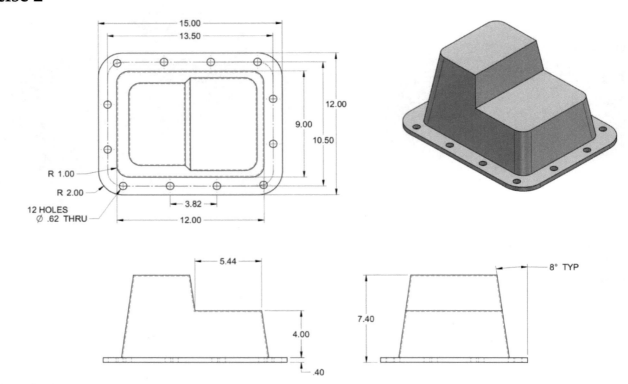

SHEET THICKNESS = 0.079 in

Chapter 10: Assemblies

Tutorial 1 (Bottom-Up Assembly)

In this example, you create the assembly shown below.

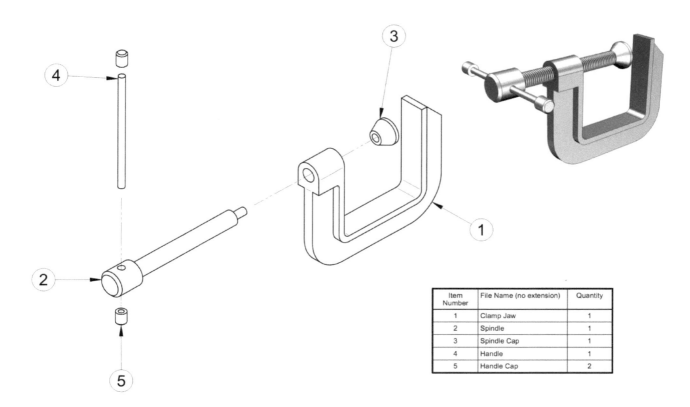

Item Number	File Name (no extension)	Quantity
1	Clamp Jaw	1
2	Spindle	1
3	Spindle Cap	1
4	Handle	1
5	Handle Cap	2

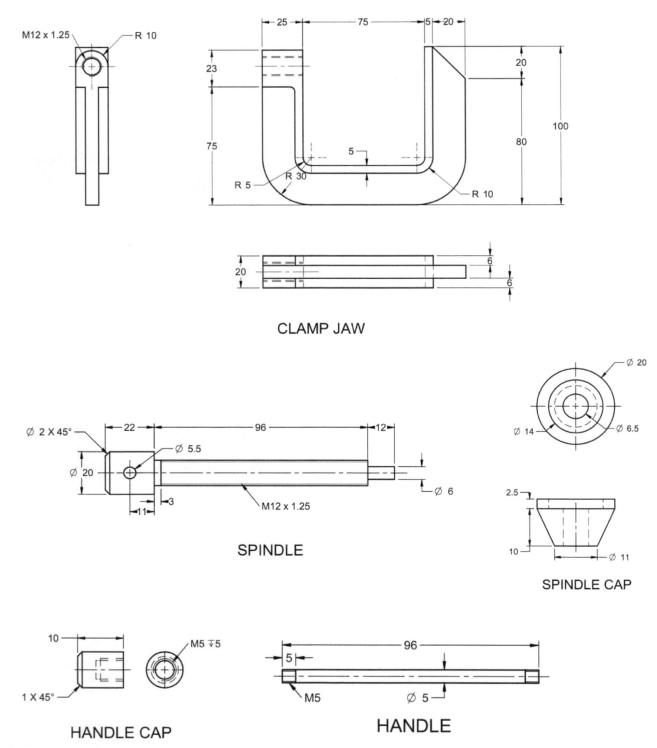

CLAMP JAW

SPINDLE

SPINDLE CAP

HANDLE CAP

HANDLE

Creating the Part files

1. In your Internet Browser, go to https://www.onshape.com to start Onshape.

2. Next, click **SIGN IN** button located on the top right corner side of the web page. Enter the username and password, and then, click **Sign in**.
3. On the Documents page, click **Create > Folder**. Next, type Chapter 10 in the **Folder name** box and then click **Create**.
4. Click on the **Chapter 10** folder in the **Folders** section.
5. On the Documents page, click **Create > Folder**.
6. Enter **Tutorial 1** in the **Folder name** box and click **Create**.
7. Click on the **Tutorial 1** folder.
8. Create all the parts of the assembly. You can also download the part files from the companion website.

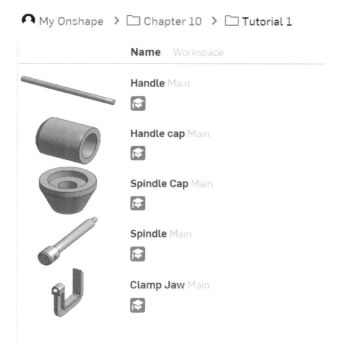

9. On the Documents page, click **Create > Document**; the **New document** dialog appears on the screen.
10. Enter **Tutorial 1** in the **Document name** box and click **OK**.
11. Click the **Document menu** located at the top left corner of the window and select **Workspace Units**; the **Workspace Units** dialog appears on the screen.
12. On the **Workspace Units** dialog, select **Default length unit > Millimeter** and **Default mass unit > Gram**.
13. Leave the other default settings and click the green check ☑.

Inserting part files in the Assemblies

1. Click the **Assembly 1** tab at the bottom of the graphics area.

2. On the toolbar, click **Insert parts and assemblies** 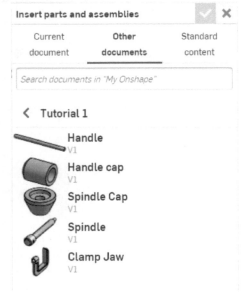 command; the **Insert parts and assemblies** dialog appears.
3. On the **Insert parts and assemblies** dialog, click the **Other documents** tab and select **My Onshape** from the
4. Expand **Chapter 10** and then click the **Tutorial 1** folder.
5. Select the **Clamp Jaw** part file from the list; a message appears that the part is not versioned.
6. Click the **Create a version in Clamp Jaw** link, and then click the **Create** button; a new version of the **Clamp Jaw** part file is created.
7. Likewise, create version files for the remaining parts, as shown.

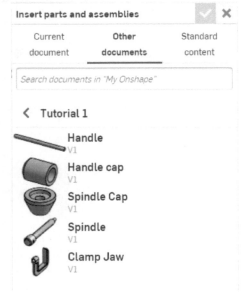

8. Select the **Clamp Jaw** file and select **Part Studio 1**. Next, click in the graphics area to place the clamp jaw.
9. Next, right click on the **Clamp jaw** in the graphics area and select **Fix**; the part is fixed at its position.

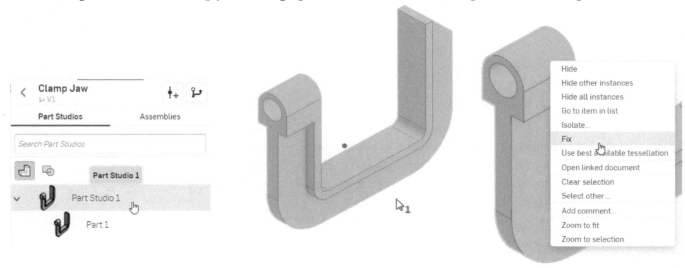

10. On the **Insert part and assemblies** dialog, click the arrow button next to Clamp Jaw.
11. On the **Insert parts and assemblies** dialog, click *Spindle*, and then click **Part Studio 1**. Click in the graphics area to place the component.

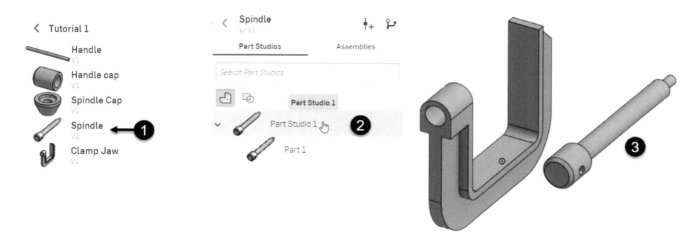

12. Likewise insert the *Spindle Cap*, *Handle*, and two instances of *Handle Caps*. Next, click the green check on the **Insert parts and assemblies** dialog.

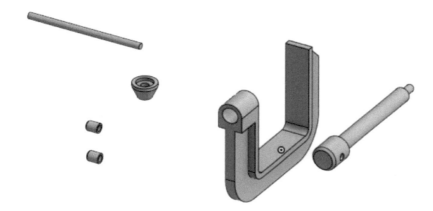

Adding the Cylindrical mate

1. On the toolbar, click the **Cylindrical mate** ⊕ command.
2. Select the circular edge of the *Spindle* and the *Clamp Jaw*.

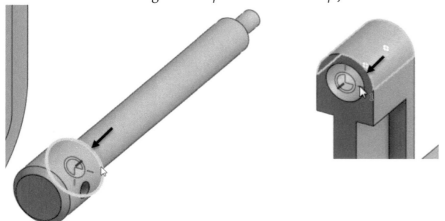

3. On the **Cylindrical 1** dialog, check the **Limit** option.

4. Type-in **-31** and **-16** in the **Limit Z minimum distance** and **Limit Z maximum distance** boxes, respectively. Next, click the green check on the dialog.

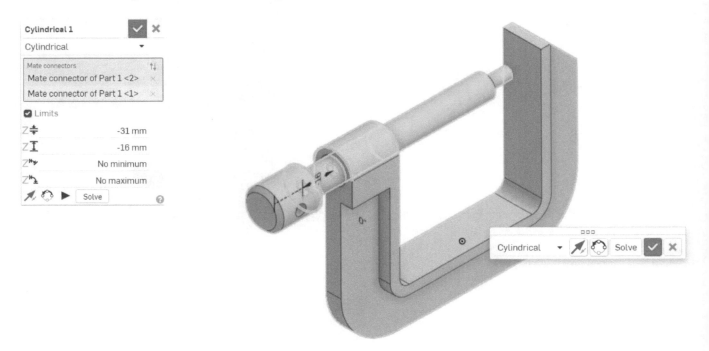

Adding the Fastened mate

1. Click the **Fastened mate** command on the toolbar.
2. Click on the circular edge of the *Spindle Cap* hole, as shown.
3. Click on the circular edge of the *Spindle*, as shown; the *Spindle* and *Spindle Cap* are axially aligned and positioned opposite to each other.
4. Click the green check on the **Fastened 1** dialog.

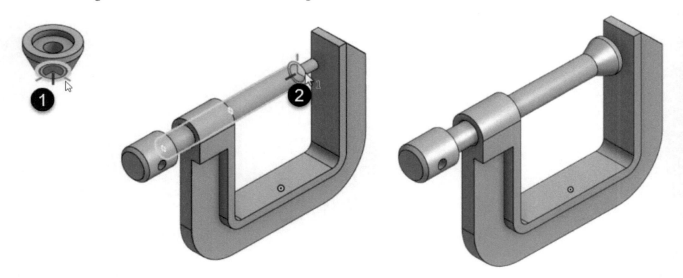

Adding the Slide mate

1. On the toolbar, click the **Slide mate** command.

2. Place the pointer at the midpoint of the *Handle* and select the Mate connector located at the midpoint.
3. Zoom-in to the hole of the *Spindle* and place the pointer on the hole. Next, move the pointer to the midpoint of the hole, and then select the Mate connector located at the midpoint.

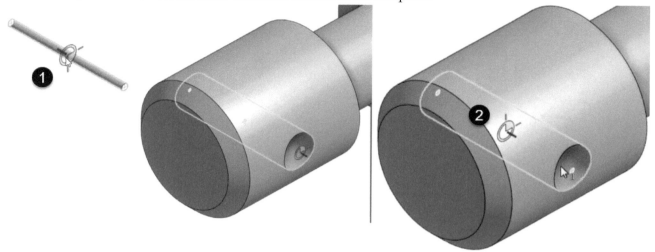

4. On the **Slider 1** dialog, check the **Limit** option.
5. Type-in **-32** and **32** in the **Limit Z minimum distance** and **Limit Z maximum distance** boxes, respectively.
6. Click the **Animate mate degrees of freedom** ▶ icon located at the bottom of the **Slider 1** dialog. Next, click the green check on the dialog.

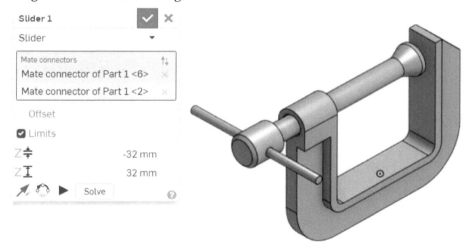

Adding the Revolute mate

1. On the toolbar, click the **Revolute mate** 🔄 command.
2. Zoom to the hole of the *Handle Cap*, and then place the pointer on the hole. Next, move the pointer and select the Mate connector located at the bottom edge of the hole, as shown.

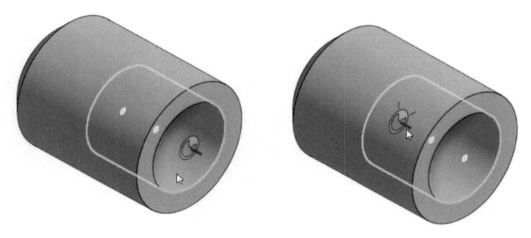

3. Select the circular edge of the *Handle*, as shown. Next, click the **Flip primary axis** icon on the **Revolute 1** dialog.

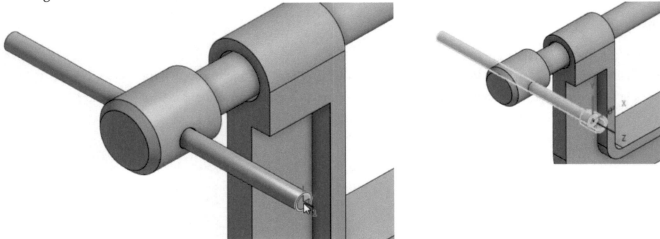

4. Click the **Animate mate degrees of freedom** ▶ icon located at the bottom of the **Revolute 1** dialog. Next, click the green check on the dialog.

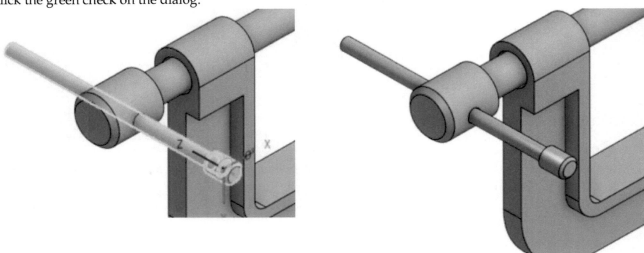

5. Likewise, insert and joint *Handle Cap* on the other side of the *Handle*.

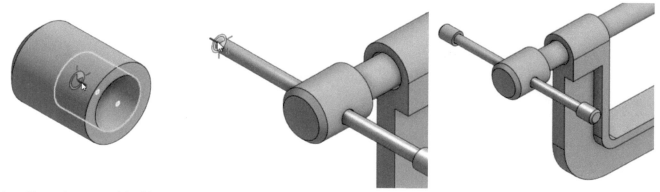

6. Close the assembly file.

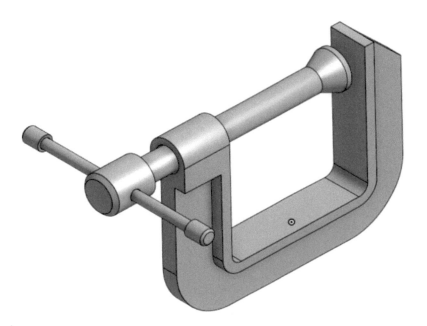

Tutorial 2 (Top-Down Assembly)

In this example, you create the assembly shown below.

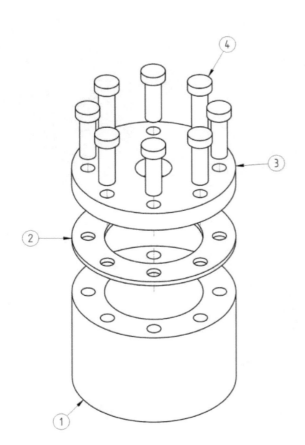

Item Number	File Name (no extension)	Quantity
1	Cylinder base	1
2	Gasket	1
3	Cover plate	1
4	Screw	8

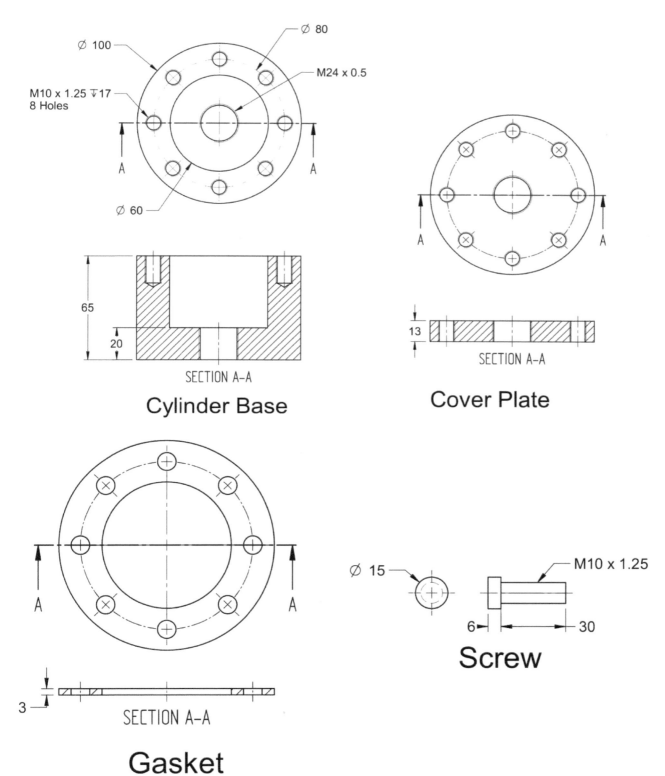

∅ 80

∅ 100

M24 x 0.5

M10 x 1.25 ⊽17
8 Holes

∅ 60

65

20

SECTION A-A

Cylinder Base

13

SECTION A-A

Cover Plate

∅ 15

M10 x 1.25

6   30

Screw

3

SECTION A-A

Gasket

Creating a New document

1. In your Internet Browser, go to https://www.onshape.com to start Onshape.

2. Next, click **SIGN IN** button located on the top right corner side of the web page. Enter the username and password, and then, click **Sign in**.
3. Click on the **Chapter 10** folder in the **Folders** section.
4. On the Documents page, click **Create > Folder**.
5. Enter **Tutorial 2** in the **Folder name** box and click **Create**.
6. Click on the **Tutorial 2** folder.
7. On the Documents page, click **Create > Document**; the **New document** dialog appears on the screen.
8. Enter *Pressure Cylinder* in the **Document name** box and click **OK**; a new document appears.
9. Click the **Document menu** located at the top left corner of the window and select **Workspace Units**; the **Workspace Units** dialog appears on the screen.
10. On the **Workspace Units** dialog, select **Default length unit > Millimeter** and **Default mass unit > Gram**.
11. Leave the other default settings and click the green check ✅.
12. Click the **Part Studio 1** tab at the bottom of the graphics area.
13. Create a *Cylinder Base* by following the steps illustrated in the figure.

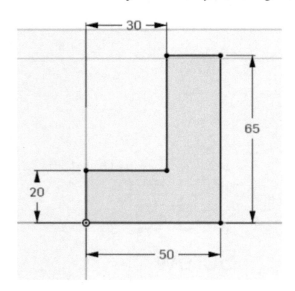

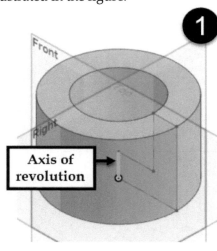

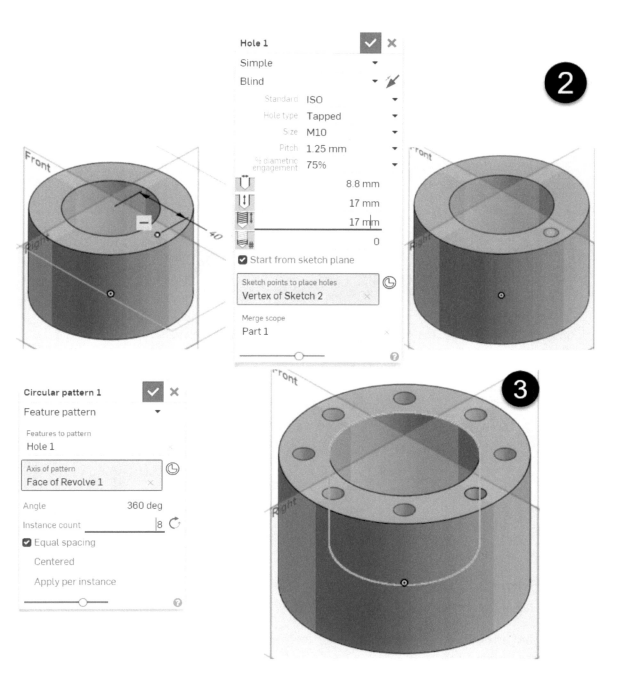

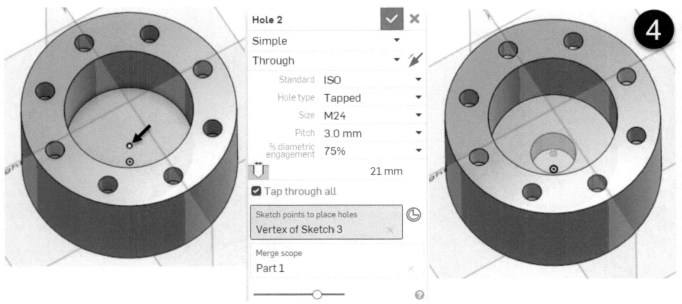

14. Right click on **Part 1** located at the bottom of the **Instances** window, and then select **Rename**.
15. Type **Cylinder Base** in the **Rename** dialog and click the green check.

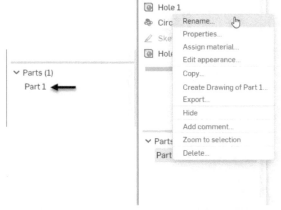

Inserting the Part into the Assembly

1. Click the **Assembly 1** tab at the bottom of the graphics area.

2. Click the **Insert parts and assemblies** command on the toolbar. Next, click the **Current document** tab on the **Insert parts and assemblies** dialog.

3. Expand **Part Studio 1** from the list, and then select Part 1. Next, click the green check on the dialog.

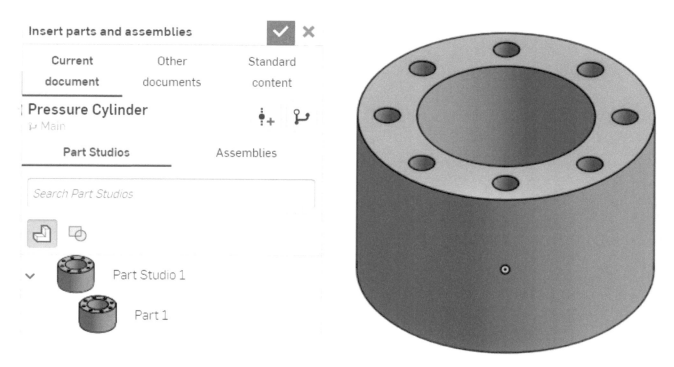

4. Right-click on the Cylinder Base and select **Fix**; the *Cylinder base* is fixed at the same place.

Creating the Mate connector

1. Click the **Mate connector** ⬡ command on the toolbar and select the center point of the top face of the model, as shown.
2. Click the green check on the **Mate connector 1** dialog to create the mate connector.

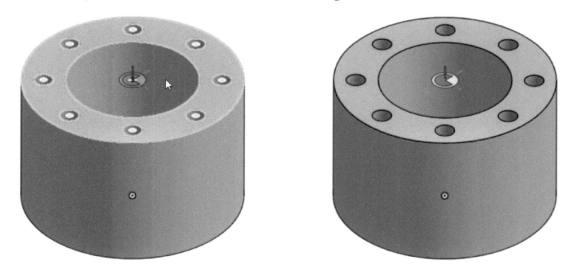

Creating Part Studios in context to the Assembly

1. Click the **Create Part Studio in context** ⬚ command on the toolbar.
2. Select the newly created mate connector and click the green check on the **Origin of new Part Studio** dialog; the **Part Studio** environment appears.

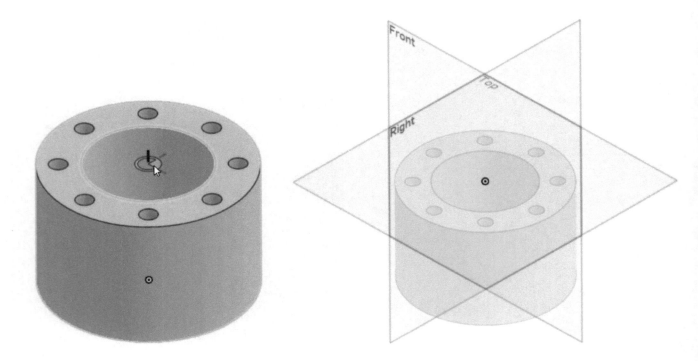

3. On the Toolbar, click the **Sketch** command. Next, select the Top face of the *Cylinder Base*.

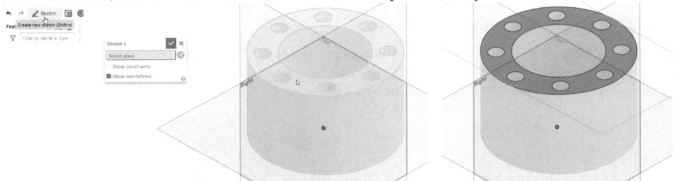

4. On the toolbar, click the **Use(project/convert)** command.
5. Click on the all circular edges on the top face of the *Cylinder Base*. The edges are projected to the sketch plane.
6. Click the green check on the **Sketch1** dialog.

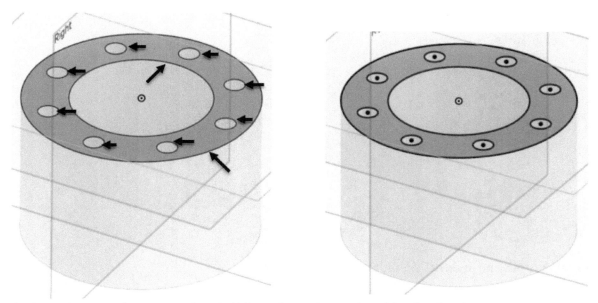

7. Activate the **Extrude** command and click on the region enclosed by the sketch.
8. On the **Extrude** dialog, click the **New** tab.
9. Select **End type > Blind**. Type 3 mm in the **Depth** field. Click the green check to create the *Extruded* feature.

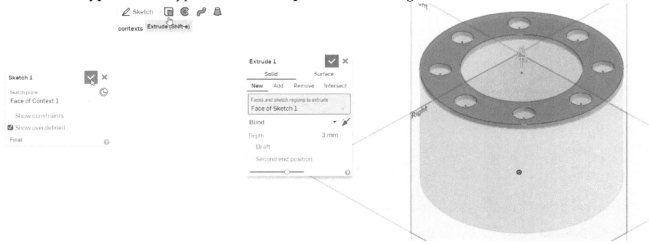

10. Right click on **Part 1** located at the bottom of the **Instances** window, and then select **Rename**.
11. Type **Gasket** in the **Rename** dialog and click the green check.
12. In the graphics area, click the **Context 1 of Assembly 1** drop-down and select **Insert and go to assembly** option. Next, click the green check on the **Select items to insert** dialog to switch to Assembly environment.
13. Click the **Mate connector** command on the toolbar8 and select the center point of the top face of the model, as shown.
14. Click the green check on the **Mate connector 2** dialog to create the mate connector.
15. Click the **Create Part Studio in context** command on the toolbar.
16. Select the newly created mate connector and click the green check on the **Origin of new Part Studio** dialog; the **Part Studio** environment appears.

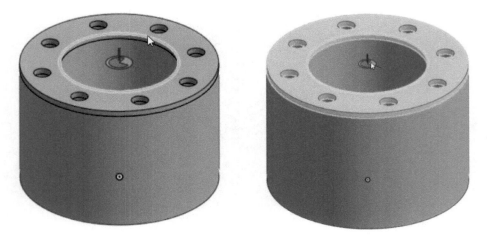

17. Activate **Sketch** command and click on the top face of the *Gasket*.

18. On the toolbar, click the **Use(project/convert)** ⬜ command.

19. Click on the outer and small circular edges of the *Gasket*; the edges are projected to the sketch plane.

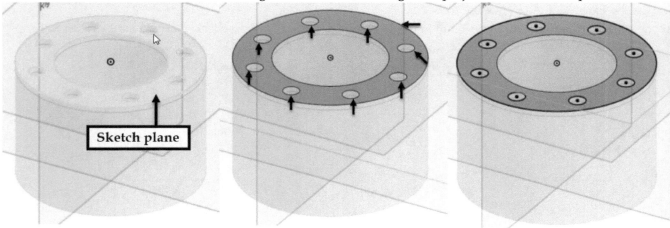

20. Click the green check on the **Sketch** dialog to confirm the sketch.

21. Click the **Extrude** ⬛ command on the toolbar and click the regions enclosed by the sketch, as shown.

22. Type 13 in the **Depth** box and click the green check on the **Extrude 1** dialog.

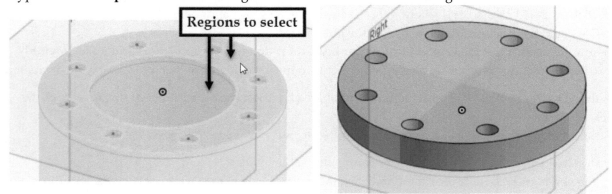

23. Create a hole in the center point of the *Cover plate*, as shown.

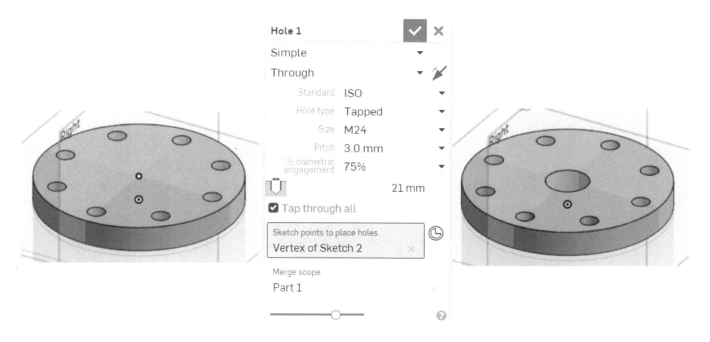

24. Right click on **Part 1** located at the bottom of the **Instances** window, and then select **Rename**.
25. Type **Cover Plate** in the **Rename** dialog and click the green check.
26. Click **Insert and go to assembly** on the **Context 1 of Assembly1** drop-down. Next, click the green check on the **Select items to insert** dialog to switch to Assembly environment.
27. Click the **Mate connector** ⓒ command on the toolbar and select the center point of any one of the small holes, as shown.
28. Click the green check on the **Mate connector 3** dialog to create the mate connector
29. In the **Instances** window, right-click on **Origin** and select **Create Part Studio in context**.
30. Select the mate connector created in the previous step. Next, click the green check on the **Origin of new Part Studio** dialog.

31. On the toolbar, click **Sketch** command and click on the top face of the *Cover Plate*.

32. On the toolbar, click the **Use(project/convert)** command and select any one of the circular edges of the holes. Click the green check on the **Sketch** dialog.

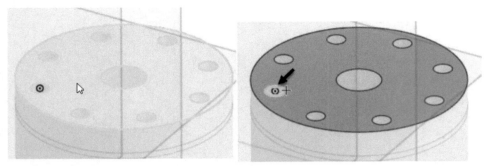

33. Use the sketch and create an *Extrude* feature of 30 mm depth. The direction of extrusion should be downward.

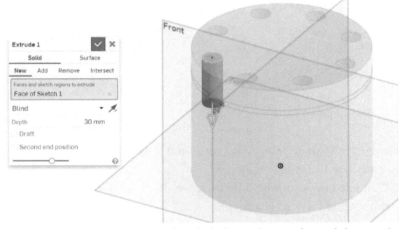

34. Activate the **Sketch** command and click on the top face of the newly created *Extruded* feature.
35. Draw a circle of 15 mm diameter and make it concentric to the circular edge of the *Extrude* feature. Click the green check on the **Sketch 2** dialog.
36. Extrude the circle in the upward direction. The extrude depth is 6 mm.

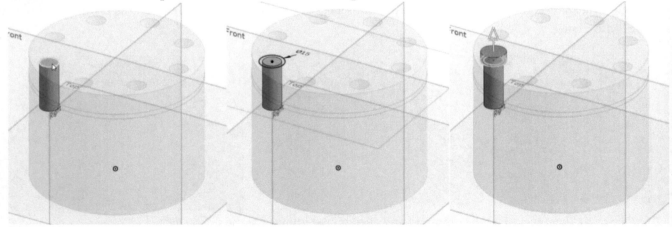

37. Right click on **Part 1** located at the bottom of the **Instances** window, and then select **Rename**.
38. Type **Screw** in the **Rename** dialog and click the green check.
39. Click **Context 1 of Assembly** drop-down > **Insert and go to assembly**. Next, click the green check on the **Select items to insert** dialog to switch to Assembly environment.

Creating the Assembly circular pattern

1. On the Toolbar, click the **Assembly circular pattern**  command.
2. Select the *Screw* from the model geometry.
3. On the **Circular pattern** dialog, click the **Axis of pattern** selection box and click on the outer circular face of the *Cover Plate*, as shown.

4. Type **360** in the **Angle** field and type in **8** in the **Instance count** field.
5. Click the green check to create the circular pattern of screws.

Creating the Named Positions

1. On the toolbar, click the **Named positions** command. Next, type Assembled view in the *New position name* box, and then click the **Add position** button next to it; a new named position is created.

2. Close the **Named positions** dialog.
3. Select the anyone of the screws from the assembly; the move triad appears on the selection.
4. Click on the axis pointing in the upward direction. Next, press and hold the left mouse button, drag it upward, and then release.
5. Type **100** in the **Distance** box that appears on the screen. Next, press Enter to move all the screws to the specified distance.

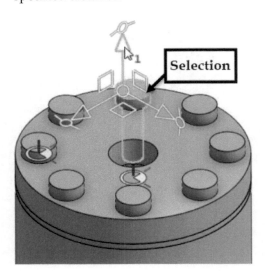 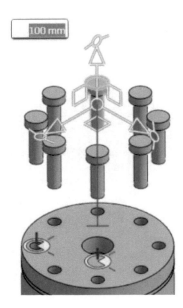

6. Click in the graphics area to deactivate the **Move** command.
7. Likewise, move the Cover plate and Gasket up to a distance of 50 and 25, respectively.

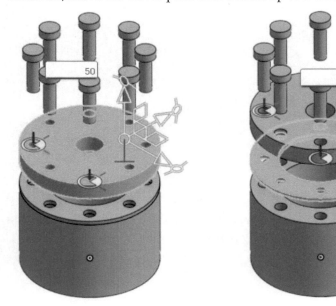 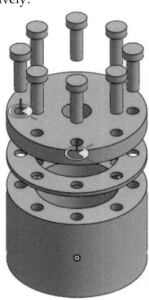

8. Click the **Named position** command on the toolbar.
9. Type Exploded view in the *New position name* box, and then click the **Add position** button. Next, select the **Exploded view** position from the drop-down located at the bottom of the **Named positions** dialog.

10. Select the **Assembly view** position from the drop-down located at the bottom of the Named positions dialog; the assembly is collapsed.

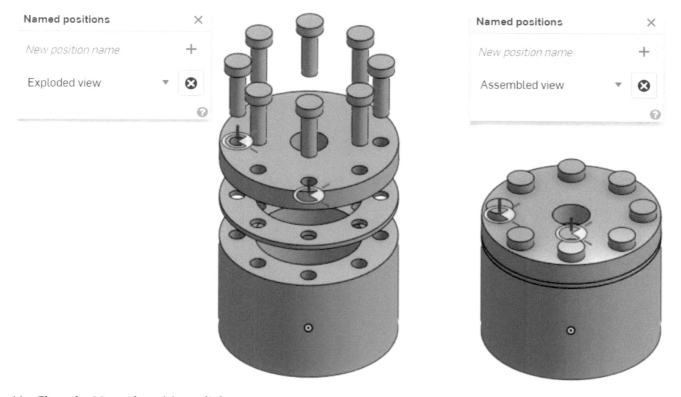

11. Close the **Named positions** dialog.

Configuring the BOM Table

1. Click the **BOM Table** button located at the right side of the graphics area; the **Bill of materials** table appears.
2. On the **Bill of materials** table, right click on the **Part number** column. Next, select **Remove column**; **the Part number** column is removed.

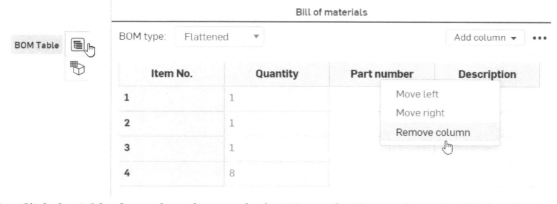

3. Click the **Add column** drop-down and select **Name**; the **Name** column is added to the table.
4. Right click on the **Name** column and select **Move left**.
5. Click the **BOM Table** button to hide the **Bill of materials** table.

6. Close the document.

Exercises
Exercise 1

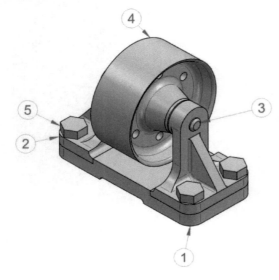

Item Number	File Name (no extension)	Quantity
1	Base	1
2	Bracket	2
3	Spindle	1
4	Roller-Bush assembly	1
5	Bolt	4

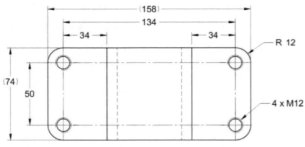

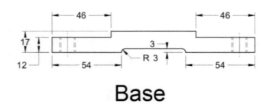

Base

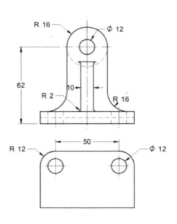
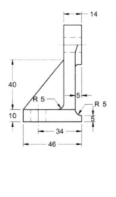

Bracket

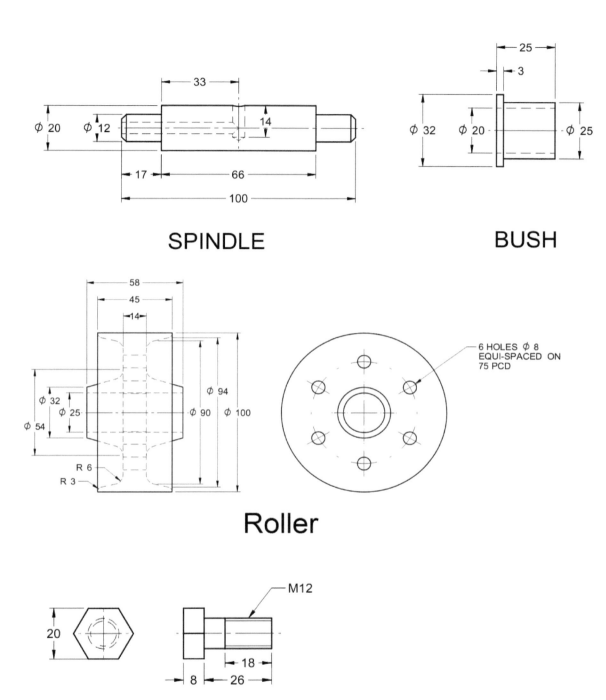

SPINDLE

BUSH

Roller

Bolt

Chapter 11: Drawings

Tutorial 1

In this example, you create the 2D drawing of the part shown below.

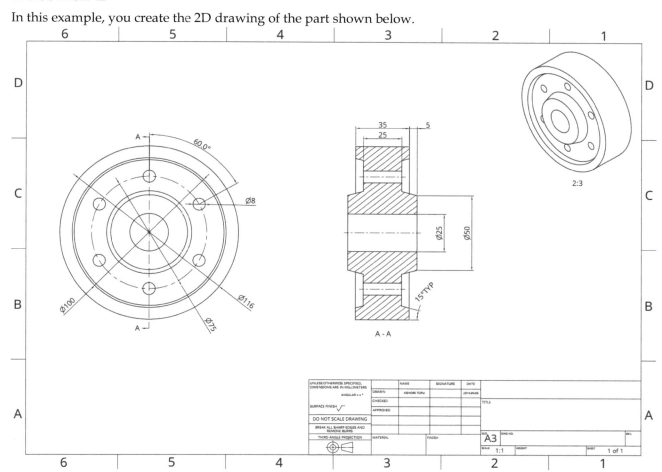

Creating a New Drawing

1. Download the **Chapter 11** part files from the companion website. Next, extract the zip file.
2. In your Internet Browser, go to https://www.onshape.com to start Onshape.

3. Next, click **SIGN IN** button located on the top right corner side of the web page. Enter the username and password, and then, click **Sign in**.
4. On the Documents page, click **Create > Folder**. Next, type Chapter 11 in the **Folder name** box and then click **Create**.
5. Double-click on the **Chapter 11** folder in the **Folders** section.
6. On the Documents page, Click **Create > Import Files** and select the **Tutorial 1** part file from the extracted zip folder. Next, click **Open** to import the selected file.
7. Double click on the imported document to open it.

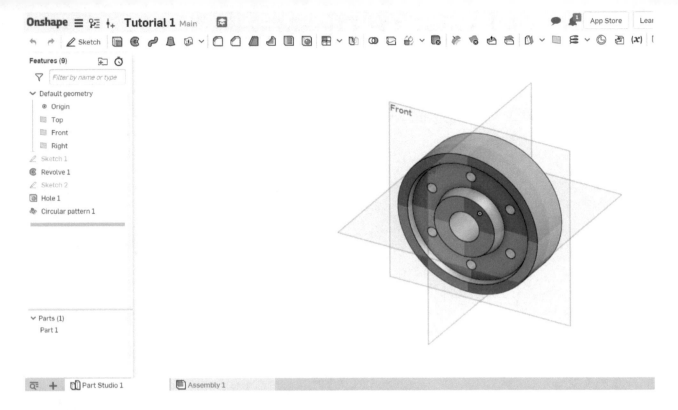

8. Click the **Insert new element** button located at the bottom left corner of the window. Next, select **Create Drawing** from the menu.

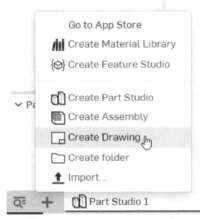

9. On the **Create Drawing** dialog, click the **Custom template** tab to create a custom template.
10. Select the **Standard > ISO** and then select **Size > A3**.
11. Select the **Units > Millimeters** and then select **Decimal separator > Period (12.34)**.
12. Select **Projection > Third angle (ANSI)**.
13. In the **Borders** section on the right side of the dialog, click **Include** option to include the border in the drawing sheet.
14. Select **Horizontal zones > 6** and **Vertical zones > 4**.
15. Click **Start zones > Bottom right** and **Titleblock > Include**.
16. Click **OK** to create a custom template and start a new drawing file.

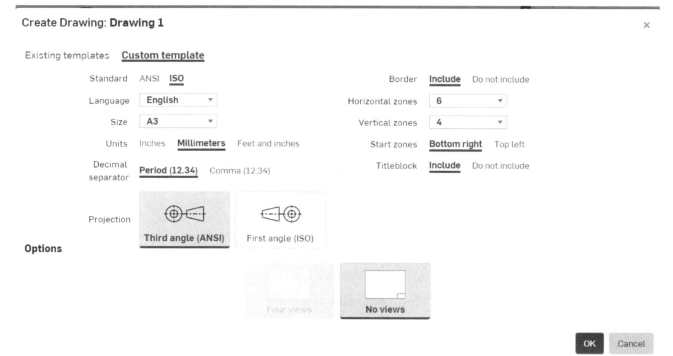

Create Drawing: **Drawing 1**

Existing templates   **Custom template**

Standard	ANSI **ISO**
Language	**English** ▾
Size	**A3** ▾
Units	Inches **Millimeters** Feet and inches
Decimal separator	**Period (12.34)** Comma (12,34)

Border	**Include** Do not include
Horizontal zones	6 ▾
Vertical zones	4 ▾
Start zones	**Bottom right** Top left
Titleblock	**Include** Do not include

Projection — **Third angle (ANSI)**   First angle (ISO)

Options

Four views   **No views**

OK   Cancel

---

17. Select **Part 1** from the **Select a part or assembly** dialog.

Inserting Drawing Views

1. On the **Insert view** dialog, select **View > Front**. Next, select **View scale > 1:1**.
2. Click on the drawing sheet at the location, as shown.

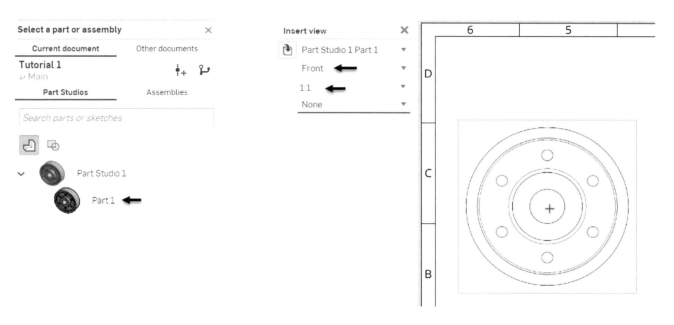

3. Move the pointer toward top right corner and click to position the isometric view, as shown.
4. Press Esc to deactivate the **Projected view** command.
5. Click and drag the Isometric view to the location, as shown.

155

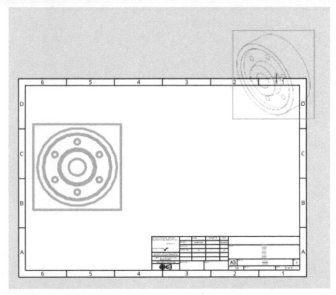

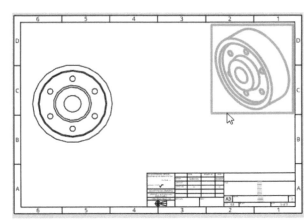

6. Double-click on the Isometric view; the **View properties** dialog appears.
7. On the **View properties** dialog, type **2:3** in the **Scale** box and click the green check.

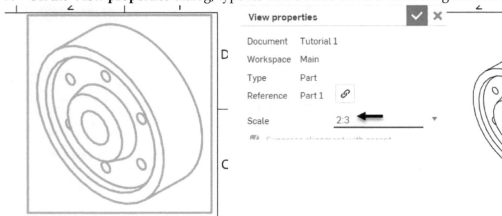

Creating the Section view

1. Activate the **Section view** command (click the **Section view** ⌇ icon on the Toolbar) and click the **Vertical** tab on the **Section View** dialog.

2. Select the center point of the front view. Next, click the **Opposite direction** ⬈ button on the **Section view** dialog.

3. Move the mouse pointer towards the right and click to position the section view.

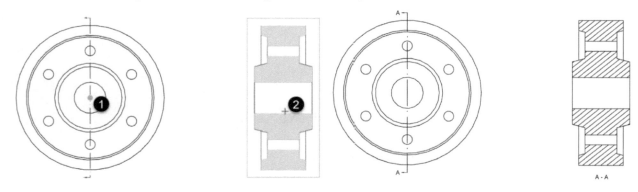

4. Activate the **Edge to edge centerline** command (click the **Edge to edge centreline** ⟩ icon on the toolbar).

5. Select the two edges on the section view, as shown. The centreline is created between the two selected edges.
6. Likewise, create two more centrelines, as shown.

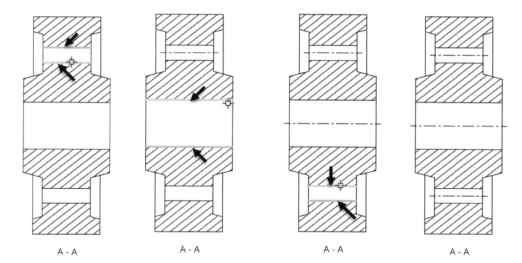

A - A   A - A   A - A   A - A

7. Activate the **3 point circle centerline** command (click the **3 point circle centreline** icon on the Toolbar) and click on the center point of the small hole at the top.
8. Likewise, select the remaining two center points of the small holes, as shown. The centreline is created between the three selected holes.

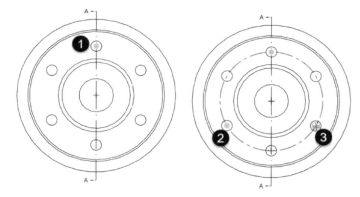

9. Click the **Centermark** command on the toolbar and select the inner circular edge of the front view.

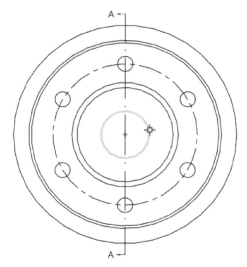

Adding Dimensions

Now, you add the dimensions to the drawing views.

1. Click **Dimension** drop-down > **2 point linear dimension** on the Toolbar.
2. Select the two points of the section view, as shown. Next, move the pointer upwards and click to add dimension.

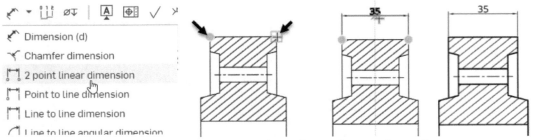

3. Click **Dimension** drop-down > **Point to line dimension** on the toolbar.
4. Select the corner point and the line of the section view, as shown. Next, move the point and place the dimension, as shown.

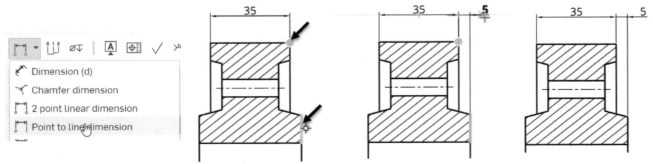

5. Click **Dimension** drop-down > **Line to line dimension** on the toolbar.
6. Select the two parallel edges of the section view, as shown. Next, move the pointer upward and click to position the dimension.

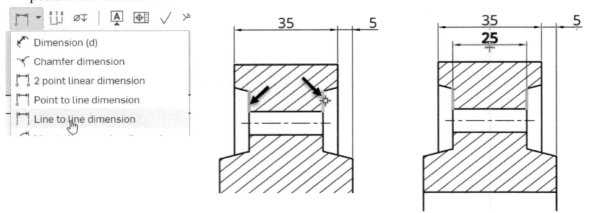

7. Click the **Dimension** command on the toolbar and select the two horizontal edges of the section view, as shown.
8. Move the pointer toward the right and click to position the dimension.
9. Place the pointer on the tolerance button that appears next to the dimension. Next, click the Insert symbol drop-down and select the diameter symbol.
10. Click in the graphics area.

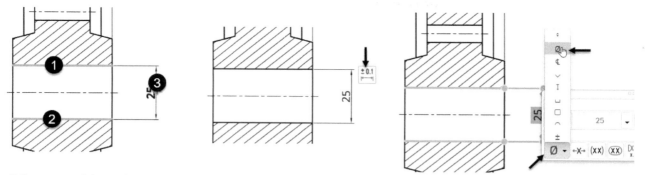

11. Likewise, add another dimension to the section view, as shown.

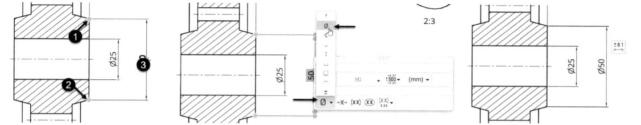

12. Click **Dimension** drop-down > **Line to line angular dimension** on the toolbar. Next, select the two edges of the section view, as shown.

13. Move the pointer toward the right and click to position the angular dimension. Next, click the tolerance button that appears next to the dimension.

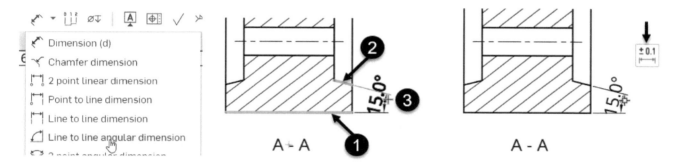

14. Click the **Precision** drop-down and select 0. Next, type **TYP** in the box next to the **Precision** drop-down.

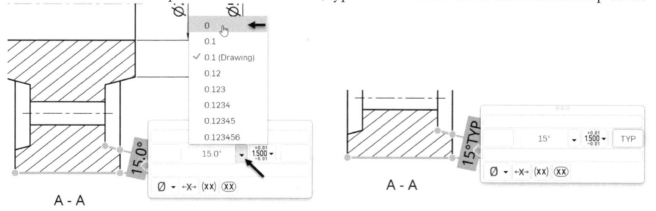

15. Click in the graphics area, and then press Esc. Next, click and drag the angular dimension, as shown.

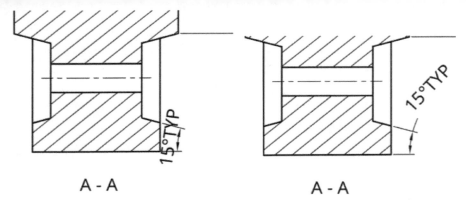

A - A   A - A

16. Click **Dimension** drop-down > **Diameter dimension** on the toolbar. Next, select the outer circular edge, as shown.
17. Move the pointer and click to position the dimension at the location, as shown.
18. Likewise, create another diameter dimension, as shown.

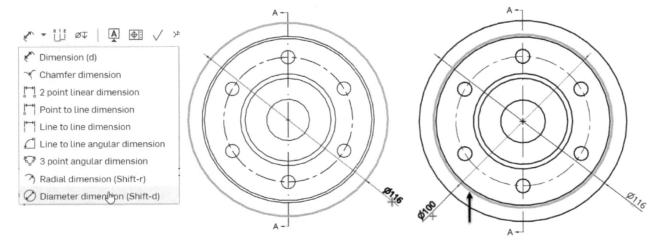

19. Activate the **Dimension** command (click the **Dimension** icon on the toolbar) and select the small hole on the front view, as shown.
20. Move the pointer diagonally and click to place the diameter dimension.
21. Likewise, apply the diameter dimension to the centerline passing through the small holes.

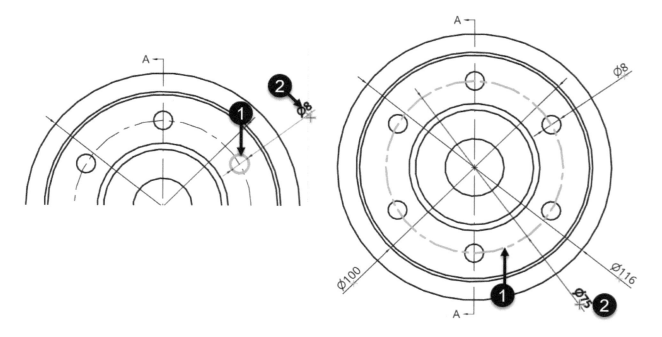

22. Click **Dimension** drop-down > **3 point angular dimension** on the toolbar. Next, select the centerpoint of the circle located at the center of the front view.

23. Select the center points of the two circles, as shown. Next, move the pointer outward and click to position the angular dimension.

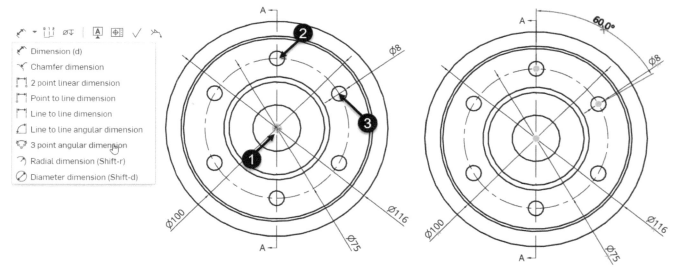

24. Click the **Document menu** located at the top left corner of the graphics area and select **Close document** to close the document.

Tutorial 2

In this example, you create an assembly drawing shown below.

Item No.	Quantity	Name	Description
1	1	Cylinder Base	
2	1	Gasket	
3	1	Cover Plate	
4	8	Screw	

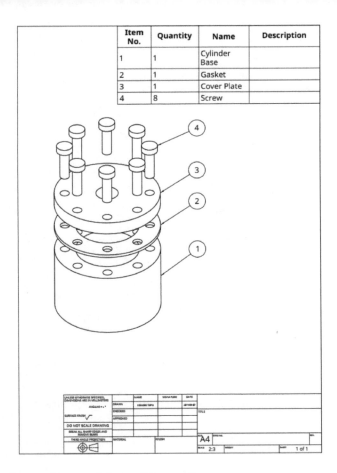

Creating a New Drawing

1. In your Internet Browser, go to https://www.onshape.com to start Onshape.

2. Next, click **SIGN IN** button located on the top right corner side of the web page. Enter the username and password, and then, click **Sign in**.
3. Double-click on the **Chapter 11** folder in the **Folders** section.
4. On the Documents page, Click **Create > Import Files** and select the **Tutorial 2** part file from the extracted Chapter 11 zip folder. Next, click **Open** to import the selected file.
5. Double click on the imported document to open it.

↶ ↷ 🖥 Insert ◒ 🛢 ⟷ 🗂 ⊕ ⟳ ♨ ⊕ ⋈ ⤵ 🔲 ⭐ 🔰 🗂 🔲 ⚙

Instances (5)

- ⊙ Origin
- 🗊 Pressure Cylinder <2>
- 🗊 Gasket <3>   ⇐
- 🗊 Cover Plate <1> ⇐
- 🗊 Screw <4>   ⇐
- › ⚙ Circular pattern 1
- ⌄ Mate Features (2)
  - 🕒 Mate connector 1
  - 🕒 Mate connector 2

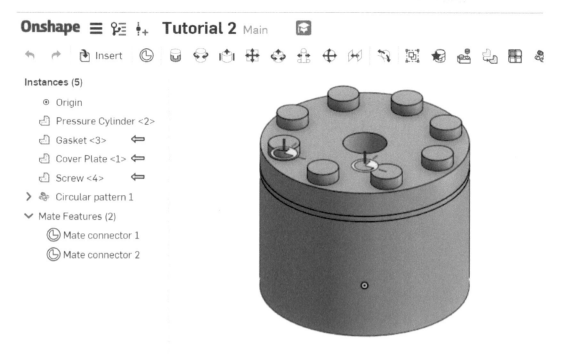

6. Select the **Exploded view** position from the drop-down located at the bottom of the **Named positions** dialog; the assembly is exploded.
7. Close the **Named positions** dialog.
8. Click the **Insert new element** button located at the bottom left corner of the window. Next, select **Create Drawing** from the menu.

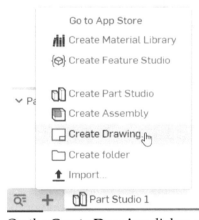

Go to App Store
- ▥ Create Material Library
- {Θ} Create Feature Studio

- ◫ Create Part Studio
- ▣ Create Assembly
- ▫ Create Drawing ⤵
- ▢ Create folder
- ⬆ Import...

Q̄ + ◫ Part Studio 1

9. On the **Create Drawing** dialog, click the **Custom template** tab to create a custom template.
10. Select the **Standard > ISO** and then select **Size > A4 Portrait**.
11. Select the **Units > Millimeters** and then select **Decimal separator > Period (12.34)**.
12. Select **Projection > Third angle (ANSI)**.
13. In the **Borders** section on the right side of the dialog, click **Include** option to include the border in the drawing sheet.
14. Click **OK** to create a custom template and start a new drawing file.
15. Click on the **Assemblies** tab and select the **Assembly 1** from the **Select a part or assembly** dialog.
16. On the **Insert view** dialog, select **View > Isometric**. Next, type **2:3** in the **View scale** box.
17. Click on the drawing sheet at the location, as shown.
18. Press Esc to deactivate the **Projected View** command.

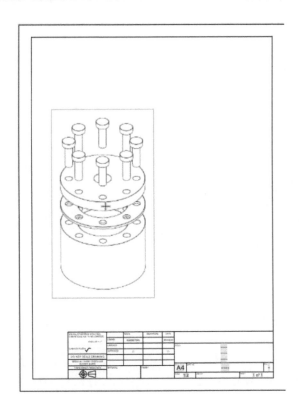
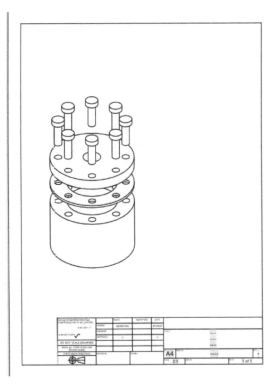

Creating the Bill of materials and Callouts

1. Click the **Insert BOM** 🖼 command on the toolbar. Next, select the top right corner ⊞ button from the **Select fixed corner** section on the **Insert BOM** dialog.

2. Select the top right corner of the sheet border; the Bill of materials table is placed at the selected point.

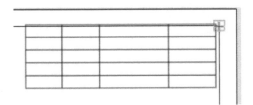

Item No.	Quantity	Name	Description
1	1	Pressure Cylinder	
2	1	Gasket	
3	1	Cover Plate	
4	8	Screw	

3. Place the pointer on the column edge of the **Description** column.

4. Press and hold the left mouse button and drag the pointer toward left; the **Description** column width is changed.

Item No.	Quantity	Name	Description
1	1	Pressure Cylinder	
2	1	Gasket	
3	1	Cover Plate	
4	8	Screw	

Item No.	Quantity	Name	Description
1	1	Pressure Cylinder	
2	1	Gasket	
3	1	Cover Plate	
4	8	Screw	

5. Likewise, change the column width of the **Quantity** column.

Item No.	Quantity	Name	Description
1	1	Pressure Cylinder	
2	1	Gasket	
3	1	Cover Plate	
4	8	Screw	

Item No.	Quantity	Name	Description
1	1	Pressure Cylinder	
2	1	Gasket	
3	1	Cover Plate	
4	8	Screw	

6. On the toolbar, click the **Callouts** command.
7. On the **Callout** dialog, select **Table property** drop-down > **Item No**.
8. Select the midpoint of the vertical edge of the cylinder base to define the start point of the callout.
9. Move the pointer diagonally toward the right and click to define the balloon location.

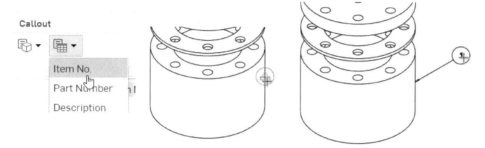

10. Select the quadrant point of the circular edge of the gasket. Next, move the pointer until a vertical tracline appears from the first balloon.
11. Click to position the balloon.
12. Likewise, add a callout to the cover plate and screw. Next, click the green check on the **Callout** dialog.

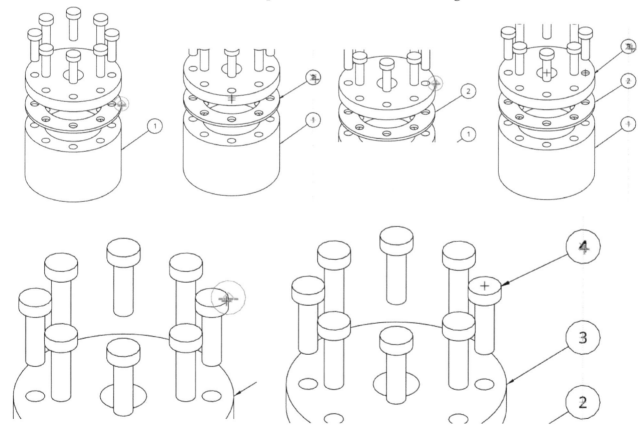

13. Close the document.

Exercises

Exercise 1

Create orthographic views of the part model shown below. Add dimensions and annotations to the drawing.

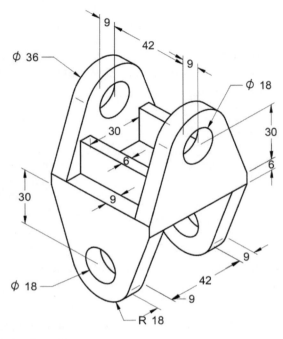

Exercise 2

Create orthographic views and an auxiliary view of the part model shown below. Add dimensions and annotations to the drawing.

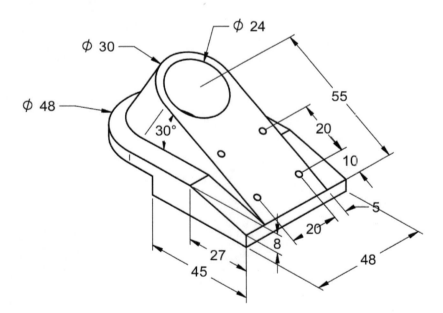

Printed in Poland
by Amazon Fulfillment
Poland Sp. z o.o., Wrocław

24010957R00101